God Bless America

EUGENE FOSS OLSEN

Acknowledgments

As a Special Agent of the Federal Bureau of Investigation (F.B.I), I served under J. Edgar Hoover for twenty-five and one half years. I also served as a Patriarch, Mission President, Temple President, and Regional Representative of The Church of Jesus Christ of Latter-day Saints. However, neither the F.B.I, nor the Church contributed in any way toward the production of this document and I alone am responsible for everything in this document.

I served for four years on the School Board of the Cajon Valley School District, San Diego County, California and, therefore, have some knowledge of schools and education. If we did not completely agree on everything, at least we knew how to disagree without being disagreeable. We probably had the most congenial school board in the State of California, and I appreciate that.

I am now over 90 years of age, a loyal and active member of The Church of Jesus Christ of Latter-day Saints and a loyal citizen of the United States of America. I am a committed disciple of Jesus Christ and son of our Father in Heaven. It is my hope, desire, and purpose to assist in the restoration of the inspired Constitution of our land and in the conversion of all the earth to the restored Church and Gospel of Jesus Christ both of which will one day be the salvation, joy, and redemption of the whole world.

I acknowledge with gratitude all the knowledge, experience and wisdom I have received from all my leaders and teachers of a whole lifetime, though at this point it is a little difficult to say exactly which bit of knowledge came from which teacher. Appreciation is expressed nonetheless for their great blessing in my life.

If, in this book, I have set forth any wisdom or knowledge that I haven't obtained through the kind teaching of others, then that would be something kindly granted to me by our Father in Heaven through the inspiration of his Holy Spirit, so I acknowledge that source also, with sincere appreciation.

Gratitude is also expressed to my wife and others who have assisted in the typing and proofreading and preparation of this book. – GOD BLESS AMERICA!

Forward

This book is copyrighted. However, anyone wanting to help correct the governmental problems herein pointed out has permission to make photocopies of this material to mail to friends, or to share this free eBook with them. If each person receiving them will send them to ten more, in six steps we will reach one million, and in ten steps everybody in the United States will know about it. **Let's do it!**

It only takes one Senator or Congressman to introduce an amendment.

GOD BLESS AMERICA!

CONTENTS

This page intentionally left blank.

CHAPTER ONE – PROPOSED AMENDMENT

Thomas Jefferson declared his greatest regret was that when the Founding Fathers set up our national government, they placed checks and balances on the Congress (the presidential veto) and on the president (Congress could over-ride his veto), *but none were placed on the Supreme Court.* They could do anything they wanted to. Let's correct that now!

On September 11, 2001, President Bush said he would ask Congress to declare war on whoever had attacked us, when they were identified. He then asked everyone to pray to God for protection and blessings, and appointed a special day for prayer services in all the churches in the nation. Then Congress and the President sang together, *"God Bless America"*.

It was refreshing to see the President move so boldly, without even asking permission of the Supreme Court, who had so totally banned God, The Bible, the Ten Commandments, and Prayer from all our schools since 1962. This contradiction of command, however, caused confusion, and two or three weeks later one woman we heard on television was particularly upset that her son now had to sing, *"God Bless America"* in school with other students, who still believe in God, which she and her son do not, since they are atheists. Her complaint was that her son's freedom of religion under the Constitution is being violated by his exposure to religious values conflicting with his own.

That, of course, is what prompted the measures taken by the Earl Warren Supreme Court in the first place. If the compulsory education laws then in effect and still in effect, violate any one's constitutional rights, why did not the Supreme Court simply declare those laws unconstitutional and send them back to Congress and the States to rewrite them? Instead, the Supreme Court proceeded to rewrite those laws themselves to correct the flaws they saw in them.

This action taken by the Supreme Court was unconstitutional. The Constitution declares that *"**ALL** legislative powers herein granted shall be invested in a **congress** of the United States which shall consist of a **Senate** and the **House of Representatives**." Nowhere in the Constitution is authorization granted to the Supreme Court to engage in any legislation whatever.*

The action taken by the Supreme Court in banning God, the Bible, the Ten Commandments and Prayer from our schools, is also a violation of the First Amendment because:

1 "Congress shall make no *law respecting an establishment of religion, or*

2. *Prohibiting the free exercise thereof...."*

If *anyone* is told where and when he can or cannot *pray*, or bring a *Bible*, or post the *Ten Commandments*, or even mention the name of God, *does this not interfere with his free exercise of religion?*

If Congress is prohibited from interfering with the free exercise of anyone's religion, *where does the Supreme Court get THEIR authority to do it?* Since it is unconstitutional to compel students to attend schools where they are exposed to religious values conflicting with their own, *why not ask Congress and the states to rewrite the law to permit parents to send their children to schools of their own choice?* They are taxpayers. Let the tax dollars go with the student.

The only people in the United States whose "freedom of religion" rights have been vigorously protected are the atheists. Does not this almost establish atheism as our State Religion? Is that not also a violation of the Constitution? And if the Supreme Court violates the very Constitution they are under oath to protect, who will declare **THAT** unconstitutional?

Some propose an amendment to permit prayer in our schools. That would be redundant. The Constitution already guarantees it and all other forms of freedom of religion as well! Our problem is that these guarantees have been suspended for the past forty years by the unconstitutional action of the Earl Warren Supreme Court.

We now hear proposals for a Judicial Constitutional Amendment, which would:

1. Absolutely forbid the Supreme Court and all federal judges from assuming any legislative powers whatever. They have none.

2. Require all Supreme Court justices and federal judges to be reconfirmed by the President and Congress, every six years.

3. Empower the President and the Congress, with a two-thirds majority, to challenge, and to veto, any action or decision of the Supreme Court or any Federal Judge, current or past.

That would provide the checks and balances on the Supreme Court that should have been established two centuries ago! That is a measure long overdue.

The Founding Fathers never intended for our Supreme Court and Federal Judges to usurp other governmental powers at will and set themselves up as a great self-appointed dictatorship to attempt to run the whole federal government as they seem determined to do now. Let's correct this at once and compel them to obey the constitution without further infractions. **Let's do it now!**

GOD BLESS AMERICA!

CHAPTER TWO – WHY TAXES?

The *only* reason for taxes, and IRS agents to collect them, is to provide the government the money it needs to operate.

Some have suggested that we now have *Congress* create our money, as the Constitution directs, instead of having the banks do it. That way we would not need either the taxes *or* the IRS to collect them. The government would already *have* the money, ready to be spent.

Much of the money could then be put into circulation through legitimate, constitutionally approved, expenditures of government. Part could also be put into circulation as a *loan* to the banks, *at* interest. That interest would help pay the cost of government, as taxes do now.

Without taxes consuming nearly half of all we earn, we would soon be saving abundantly to establish businesses and plants all over the land. We could manufacture everything from lawn mowers and sewing machines to tooth brushes and shoelaces, and everything else in between.

There would be employment for everyone willing to work, and every family would have an income. Capable and intelligent citizens now collecting taxes and preparing tax returns could serve as supervisors and directors in every business in the nation. Then we would *really* prosper.

Federal Reserve Chairman Alan Greenspan recently said he was raising interest rates on loans to "cool" the economy. In other words, he means, *to reduce our money.* This would avoid inflation, he says, as "too much money chasing too few goods" is what causes inflation.

Let us reverse that equation. Instead of reducing our money, let us increase our production of goods. That should balance things out a little better, and we can do it when we revise our monetary system to conform to our inspired Constitution.

When the money masters told Woodrow Wilson they could make him president if he would establish the Federal Reserve, they assured him this would end depressions and recessions forever. Adequate money would always be available, interest rates would be low, and everyone would prosper.

So they passed the *Federal Reserve Act* and *turned the creation and control of our money over to the banks, in 1913, and we've been having recessions and depressions ever since.* There would be no inflation, we were told, but today it costs from ten to twenty times as much to buy or build a house as it did when we had our first house built in 1952.

When loan interest rates reached 21%, a few years back, President Carter said, "Yes, it's terrible, but neither I nor Congress can do anything about it." That of course, is ridiculous. If Congress and the President could *pass* the Federal Reserve Act in 1913, they can *repeal* it now, or anytime they choose.

Do you know what will happen when we restore the Constitution? Go read the Preamble again and you will find out!

"We, the People of the United States, in Order to form a more perfect Union, establish Justice, insure domestic Tranquility, provide for the common defense, promote the general Welfare, and secure the Blessings of Liberty to ourselves and our Posterity, do ordain and establish this Constitution for the United States of America."

When we restore our inspired Constitution and follow it, the whole world will follow our example, for their good, and for our own. A good time to do that is now, and a good place to start is shown you above. We will be the happiest and most prosperous people on the whole Planet Earth.

Let's do it! *Have Congress create our money, abolish taxes and the IRS, and Federal Reserve and PROSPER.* That would "promote the *general* welfare," instead of only the welfare of the privileged few.

Let us get back to that inspired Constitution the way the good Lord gave it. While we are at it, let us get back to the good Lord, and we will be blessed and prospered forever.

GOD BLESS AMERICA!

CHAPTER THREE – AND TO THE REPUBLIC

The pledge of Allegiance proclaims:

I pledge Allegiance to the flag of the
United States of America
And to the Republic for which it stands,
One nation under God,
Indivisible,
With Liberty and Justice for all.

Many of those who clamored for the 17th Amendment, rejoiced in its passage, in 1913. They considered that a significant step toward changing our nation from a Republic to a Democracy. Perhaps they did not really understand the difference. Many people still do not. However, our Founding Fathers did, and they deliberately formed our government as a Republic rather than a democracy.

We usually use the word *democracy* to describe a government based on the *vote* of the governed. That, of course, is good, but our Founding Fathers felt a *Republic* was even better. In a Republic the *people* do the *voting*, and they vote for *representatives* (President, Congress, etc.), and the *representatives* do the *governing*. However, the republic they set up was a *constitutional* republic, as a double precaution. Why?

Well, let us see how this works.

To start out with, the Declaration of Independence, which serves as an introduction to our Constitution that followed, starts out by saying there is a God who was our Creator. He gave us certain *rights,* which no power on earth can take away, for they are *inalienable.*

Among our God-given inalienable rights are the right to *life, liberty,* and *the pursuit of happiness*, which would have to include the right to *work and produce property*, and the *right to enjoy that property after we got it produced.*

The Constitution was then drawn up to ensure the protection of those God-given rights from the usurpation of government. The Constitution was not created to protect the Government from the people, but to protect the *people* from their Government.

The principle danger of an unrestricted democracy is that having eliminated God from all consideration in the matter, men soon presume to be their own god, for whatever 52% of the voters declare to be right, thereby *becomes* right. For example, if the *majority* say it is right to kill an unborn baby, that makes it right. By the same token they may decide to start at the other end and eliminate the aged on the grounds that those over 90 years of age are not normally very productive members of society anyway.

It gets even worse. In his book *"The Law"*, the author, Frederic Bastiat (1801-1850), a French economist, statesman, and author writes: "The *Law* is perverted! In addition, the police powers of the State are perverted along with it! The *Law*, is not only turned from its proper purpose, but made to follow an entirely contrary purpose! The Law has become the weapon of every kind of *greed*. Instead of checking crime, the Law itself is guilty of the evils it is supposed to punish!" (p.5.)

Greedy voters vote to have the government itself do the plundering of other men's goods, which makes it *legal* plunder. Then they happily engage in dividing the spoils:

"The Law...has acted in direct opposition to its own purpose. It has been used to destroy its own objectives. It has been applied to annihilating the justice that it was supposed to maintain. The Law has placed the collective force at the disposal of the unscrupulous that wish, without risk, to exploit the person, liberty, and property of others. It has converted *plunder* into a *right,* in order to protect plunder. And it has converted lawful defense into a crime in order to punish lawful defense" (p. 9) That is the danger of unrestricted democracy, especially when motivated by socialism and greed.

Therefore, the Founding Fathers set up our government as a *republic,* drew up the Constitution to preserve and protect it, and established the Supreme Court to preserve and protect the Constitution.

Are we still running as clean as we were set up to be? Since that is the desire of our Father in Heaven. **Let's do it!**

GOD BLESS AMERICA!

CHAPTER FOUR – THE SEVENTEENTH AMENDMENT OR THE TENTH AMENDMENT?

The Declaration of Independence, declares, "We hold these truths to be self-evident, that all men are created equal, that they are endowed by their Creator *with certain inalienable Rights,* that among these are *Life, Liberty* and the *Pursuit of Happiness.*" It adds: "To secure these Rights, Governments are instituted among Men, deriving their just Powers from the Consent of the Governed."

The Founding Fathers promptly set about with zeal and enthusiasm to then establish the government that would indeed secure our rights, even the government of the United States of America. To guide them in setting up our government, and to thereafter protect the citizens *from* their Government, they laboriously drew up our entire Constitution. Nations have come and Nations have gone and their Constitutions have come and gone with them, but this Constitution and This Nation are now well into their third Century. Not only are they still intact, but also this Constitution has produced the greatest, most powerful, most wealthy, most progressive and most prosperous Nation on earth.

To control this wonderful and powerful government the Founding Fathers incorporated into its Constitution the Tenth Amendment which says: "The powers not delegated to the United States by the Constitution, nor prohibited by it to the States, *are reserved to the States respectively, or to the people.*" That means, our Federal Government holds all the powers conferred upon it by our Constitution *and none others.*

Regulating Interstate Commerce was a responsibility for the National Government since all States were involved. Immigration likewise; Federal Courts and Judges also, and especially providing for the Common Defense. Maybe they thought the States and Communities and the Citizens themselves were quite capable of teaching children to read and write and do basic math, and even to teach the farmers how to farm. *At least, nothing in the Constitution assigns the National Government to do it.*

Note how deeply the Founding Fathers wanted to keep our National Government from usurping powers that really belong to the States, the citizens, and the local communities and parents, by passage of the Tenth Amendment.

It almost appears that their formation of a bi-cameral legislature in the government, with the House of Representatives, to represent the *people* and the Senate to represent the *States,* was done deliberately as a check and balance, to make sure the Tenth Amendment was enforced. Each member of the House of Representatives was elected by the vote of the citizens of their particular congressional district. That is the way it was then, and that is the way it is now.

The Senate, though, is quite a different matter. Initially the two Senators were chosen by the legislature of their State and their principle duty in Congress was to represent the interests of their State. *Their state hired them, fired them, and determined their pay.*

With the passage of the 17th Amendment in 1913, senators are no longer appointed by their state, but are now elected by the combined voters of their whole state. *The states no longer set their pay, and the states no longer have anyone to represent them in Congress.*

The senators raise their own pay at will and everyone else's taxes to match. In addition, with the original checks and balances removed in this manner, *the Tenth Amendment has become little more than a bad joke.* How true this is can best be seen in the Republican governors' conference a couple of elections ago. The governors drafted an appeal to the federal government complaining of all the powers the federal government had usurped which the governors were demanding to be restored to the states.

Have they been returned? When they are you will probably know about it. Meanwhile some of us are beginning to wonder if the passage of the 17th Amendment has not really produced more disadvantages than advantages. *Maybe the Tenth Amendment was a greater blessing than the 17th Amendment, which has almost supplanted it!*

GOD BLESS AMERICA!

CHAPTER FIVE – A GREAT GENTILE NATION

Many have expressed amazement that a group of men such as our Founding Fathers should have been able to put together in such a short time such a document as our Constitution, capable not only of enduring for over two centuries but also able to create the most powerful, most progressive, and wealthiest nation on earth.

One author, Ray C. Hillam, political scientist, economist, and professor of law, compiled a whole book, *"By the Hands of Wise Men,"* of essays on the United States Constitution, mostly praising it. He quotes the prominent historian Henry Steele Commager:

Yet who can doubt that in the last quarter of the 18th Century it was the New World – not democracy by our standards, but certainly democracy by European standards-- that provided the most impressive spectacle of leadership, rather than the nations of the Old World? Who can doubt, for example, that in the crisis of 1774 – 1783, the American Colonies and States enjoyed far more competent leadership than the British Empire? ...

In the last quarter of the Century the new United States...with a white population of less than 3,000,000 boasted a galaxy of leaders who were quite literally incomparable: Franklin, Washington, Jefferson, Hamilton, John Adams, Samuel Adams, John Jay, James Wilson, George

Mason, Benjamin Rush, James Madison, and a dozen others scarcely less distinguished.

What explains this remarkable outpouring of political leadership, this fertility in the production of Statesmen, a fertility unmatched since that day? Was it an historical accident? Was it a peculiar response to the time or the place, or to a combination of the two? Or was it a product of conditions and attitudes that were cultivated and directed to calculated ends, and that can be if not re-created at least paralleled in our time?

Such statements testify to the writing political wisdom and leadership of American Statesmen in the 18th Century.... The American people themselves were a remarkable group...the political wisdom of the Founding Fathers ran simultaneously through the general populace.

The picture emerging today suggests that the Americans were a surprisingly literate people and their intelligent and informed interest in public affairs was extraordinary among 18th Century societies. Not a house was to be found where a newspaper was not read and there were few townships which did not possess a little library formed and supported by subscription. (Pg. 4-5)

The Book of Mormon speaks of a great gentile (non-Jewish) nation to be raised up on this land. It is obviously the United States of America. Lehi said, "Yea, the Lord hath covenanted this land unto me, and to my children forever and also all those who should be led out of other countries by the hand of the Lord.

Wherefore, I, Lehi, prophesy according to the workings of the Spirit which is in me, that *there shall none come into this land (America) save they shall be brought by the hand of the Lord.*

Wherefore, this land is consecrated unto him whom he shall bring.

And if it so be that they shall serve Him according to the commandments, which He hath given, *it shall be a land of liberty unto them. They shall never be brought down into captivity*; if so, it shall be because of iniquity; for if iniquity shall abound cursed shall be the land for their sake, *but unto the righteous it shall be blessed forever.*" (*The Book of Mormon*, II Nephi 1: 5-7, emphasis added)

In the book, "We Believe the Bible" I quoted what the Biblical Prophet Isaiah had to say about a "book" the Lord would bring forth at a time future from Isaiah's day. The Lord would bring forth that book as part of a Marvelous Work, even "A Marvelous Work and a Wonder" which the Lord would bring forth.

In *The Book of Mormon*, which claims to be the latter day "book" foretold by Isaiah, we read of a great gentile (non-Jewish) nation, which the Lord would raise up on this land of America in the latter days. The gentiles who founded it would be faithful God-fearing, Bible-reading and Bible-believing sons and daughters of our Father in Heaven, and because of their great faith and obedience to God (starting with the Ten Commandments), *they would be protected and preserved from all other nations on earth.*

They would remain blessed and protected by our Father in Heaven as long as they remain faithful to him. What about the beastly slaughter of innocent, defenseless unborn babies? What about adultery so widespread that many people do not even bother to get married anymore? Are these evidences of our not keeping the Lord's commandments?

Is the Lord still preserving and protecting us in spite of all that? I believe that He is! Two or three weeks after the 9 /11 attack on New

York City and the Pentagon my wife and I were watching Television and several preachers from Chicago told how the night before that attack they felt such great concern for Chicago that they stayed up all night praying for the protection of that City.

Chicago is where the famous Sears Tower is located and if a high-jacked plane had destroyed that it would have caused as much disorientation and confusion as was seen in New York City. However, they prayed all night for the protection of their city and it was spared. Could that have been the destination of the plane that crashed short of its goal that fateful day? If our Father in Heaven gave us even that much protection why don't we now *really* repent and get the rest of His blessings that await us when we obey the law so we can get the blessings? One revelation says, "There is a law irrevocably decreed in Heaven before the foundations of this world, upon which all blessings are predicated, and when we obtain any blessing from God it is by obedience to that law upon which it is predicated." (*Doctrine & Covenants* 130:20-21, emphasis added.)

What can we do? Well, to start with we can stop voting for evil men to be our President. What kind of blessings can we expect when our people elect for our President and Commander-in-Chief a man who is himself a draft dodger? How can we expect a man to be true to his country when he is not even true to his own wife?

What can we all do? Well, we can all vote. The Lord has said,

Verily I say unto you, my friends, fear not, let your hearts be comforted; yea, rejoice evermore, and in everything give thanks; waiting patiently on the Lord for your prayers have entered into the ears of the Lord of Sabaoth, and are recorded with this seal and testament – *the*

17

Lord has sworn and decreed that they shall be granted.

Therefore, he giveth this promise unto you, *with an immutable covenant that they shall be fulfilled;* and all things wherewith you have been afflicted shall work together for your good, and to my name's glory, saith the Lord.

And now, verily I say unto you concerning the laws of the land, it is my will that *my people shall observe to do all things whatsoever I command them. And that law of the land which is constitutional, supporting that principle of freedom in maintaining rights and privileges, belongs to all mankind, and is justifiable before me.* Therefore, I, the Lord, justify you, and your brethren of my church, in befriending that law which is the Constitutional law of the land; And as pertaining to law of man, whatsoever is more or less than this, cometh of evil.

I, the Lord God, make you free, therefore you are free indeed and the law also maketh you free. Nevertheless, when the wicked rule the people mourn. Wherefore, *honest* men and *wise* men should be sought for diligently and *good men and wise men ye should observe to uphold;* Otherwise, whatsoever is less than these cometh of evil.... *If ye observe to do whatsoever I command you, I, the Lord, will turn away all wrath and indignation from you, and the gates of hell shall not prevail against you.* (*Doctrine & Covenants* 98:1,10–22, emphasis added)

All wrath and indignation shall be turned away from us, the gates of hell shall not prevail against us, and we shall be preserved from the powers of all nations on earth, as long as we will love and serve the Lord. We are the sons and daughters of our Father in Heaven. Let us love him, serve him, and keep his commandments, starting with the basic Ten!

Blessed be the name of the Lord!

GOD BLESS AMERICA!

CHAPTER SIX – BLOWN OUT TO SEA

The Biblical prophet Isaiah and the Book of Mormon Prophet Nephi both foretold in rather full detail early American History. Nephi's father, Lehi, knew as early as 600 B.C. that the American Continent would be kept hidden for many centuries by the Lord. Otherwise, "many nations would overrun the land, that there would be no place for an inheritance." (*The Book of Mormon*, 2 Nephi 1:8)

Lehi said America was being saved to become a latter-day land of Liberty: "There shall be none come into this land save they shall be brought by the hand of the Lord. Wherefore, *this land is consecrated unto him whom He shall bring.* And if it so be that they shall serve Him according to the commandments which he hath given (including the basic Ten!), it shall be a land of liberty unto them." (*The Book of Mormon*, 2 Nephi 1:6-7, emphasis added) He then promises this great gentile nation, which is obviously the United States, the *unfailing blessings and protection and preservation of the Lord, conditioned on our obedience:*

Wherefore, "*they shall never be brought down into captivity*; if so, it shall be because of iniquity; *for if iniquity shall abound cursed shall be the land for their sakes, but unto the righteous it shall be blessed forever.*" (ibid, verse 7, emphasis added)

Nephi was shown in vision the latter-day coming of the Gentiles to America. He saw Columbus and wrote, "I beheld the Spirit of God, that it came down and wrought upon the man, and he went forth among the many waters, even unto the seed of my brethren." (The Indians in America) (*The Book of Mormon*, 1 Nephi 13:12)

He continues, "And it came to pass that I beheld the spirit of God, that it wrought upon other Gentiles; and they went forth out of captivity, upon the many waters…*and they did prosper and obtained the land for their inheritance, and the Gentiles who had gone forth out of captivity did humble themselves before the Lord; and the power of God was with them.*" (*The Book of Mormon*, 1 Nephi 13:13-16, emphasis added)

Continuing, "I, Nephi beheld that the gentiles that had gone forth out of captivity *were delivered by the power of God out of the hands of all other nations.*" (ibid. 1 Nephi 13:19, emphasis added)

In October of 1746, *the entire French fleet arrived at Boston with orders to burn it to the ground.* The colonists had no cannon, very few side arms, and no army at all. Without other means of defense, the governor called for a day of universal fasting and prayer. Everywhere the colonists obeyed it, thronging to the churches.

In Boston the reverend Thomas Prince from the high pulpit of the old South Meeting House, prayed before hundreds. The morning was clear and calm; people had walked to church through sunshine.

"Deliver us from our enemies!" the minister implored. "Send thy tempest Lord, upon the waters to the eastward! Raise thy right hand. Scatter the ships of our tormentors and drive them hence. Sink their proud frigates beneath the power of thy winds!"

He had scarcely pronounced the words until the sun was gone and the morning darkened, the wind shrieked round the walls, sudden violent, hammering at the windows with a giant hand. No man was in the steeple…but the great bell struck twice, a wild uneven sound. Thomas Prince paused in his prayer, both arms raised. "We hear thy voice, O Lord," he thundered triumphantly. "We hear it! Thy breath is upon the waters to the eastward, even upon the deep. Thy bell tolls for the death of our enemies!" He bowed his head; when he looked up tears streamed down his face. "Thine be the glory, Lord, amen and amen!" (W. Cleon Skousen "Isaiah speaks to Modern Times". Pp. 83-84, quoting from Catherine Drinker Bowen, "John Adams and the American Revolution" pp. 10-11).

The whole fleet was nearly lost, the men were very sick, and the Admiral and Vice-Admiral had committed suicide. Two thousand of their men had died and were buried, four thousand were sick and fewer than a thousand of their land forces remained, as the battered fleet limped away, and Out To Sea. They were totally routed, the Lord saved the Colonists, and not a shot was fired.

The Lord gave that promise of protection with a covenant, and he really fulfilled it!

Blessed be the name of the Lord!

GOD BLESS AMERICA!

CHAPTER SEVEN – OUR CONSTITUTION

The Lord has commanded his people to obey his law and keep all of his commandments, including the Basic Ten (*Doctrine & Covenants* 98:4-9; *Doctrine & Covenants* 59:3, 5-9)

They are also to obey, support, and befriend the "Constitutional law of the land;" The Lord explained, "and that law of the land which is constitutional...belongs to all mankind, and is justifiable before me." (*Doctrine & Covenants* 98:5) He then added, "And as pertaining to law of man, *whatsoever is more or less than this, cometh of evil.*"

Then he instructed the Saints, "I, the Lord God, make you free, therefore ye are free indeed; and the law also maketh you free. Nevertheless, when the wicked rule the people mourn. Wherefore, *honest* men and *wise* men should be sought for *diligently*, and *good men and wise men ye should observe to uphold; otherwise whatsoever is less than these cometh of evil.*" (Ibid. verses 8-10, emphasis added)

Many have felt that both our Constitution itself, and the men who wrote it were *inspired* to bring it forth. By Latter-day revelation the Lord adds: "And for this *purpose have I established* the Constitution of this land, by the hands of wise men whom I raised up unto this very purpose, and redeemed the land by the shedding of blood." (*Doctrine & Covenants* 101:80, emphasis added)

Our Constitution *was established by the Lord*, through wise men raised up by the Lord for the very purpose of writing it. The Prophet of the Restoration, Joseph Smith, said our Constitution would be rejected, abused, and disregarded, until it was left hanging "as by a single thread." He then added that at that critical juncture "the elders of this Church will step forth and save it." Let's hope they do! Otherwise, things may become a little problematical! The responsibility is ours. Let us be faithful to the Lord and we will be a blessing to our nation and to all our people!

We are to obey our Father in Heaven in all things. We are to keep all of his commandments, including the Basic Ten. He gave us our Constitution for our protection and for our guidance. We are to cherish it and sustain it. Our Supreme Court was established to see that we do, and as we maintain our Constitution, it will be a joy, a protection, and a blessing to us. It will also cause us to rejoice and prosper. Everyone will be able to work, will have a roof over their head, and will have food to eat and a good bed to sleep in.

For the past century, we have been victimized by Constitutional apostasy, and we have been so plagued by recessions, depressions, and inflation that today there are multitudes in our land who do not even have a home to live in, as Thomas Jefferson feared would be. We are in a chosen land as the Lord said we would be. The founders of our nation were God-fearing men and women. They had great faith and the Lord promised he would preserve and protect them. That is why he gave us our Constitution in the first place.

The scripture declares, "But if the Gentiles will *repent and RETURN unto me*, saith the Father, they shall be numbered among my people, O house of Israel. But if they will *not* return unto me, and hearken unto my voice, I will suffer them; yea, I will suffer my people, O house of Israel, that they shall go through among them, and they shall tread them down, and they shall be as salt that hath lost its savor, which is thenceforth good for nothing, but to be cast out, and to be trodden under foot of my people, O house of Israel. Verily, verily, I say unto you, thus hath the Father commanded me – that I should give unto this people [the seed of Lehi] this land for their inheritance.

And then the words of the prophet Isaiah shall be fulfilled, which say, Thy watchmen shall lift up the voice; with the voice together shall they sing, for they shall see eye to eye when the Lord shall bring again Zion. Break forth into joy, sing together, ye waste places of Jerusalem; for the Lord hath comforted his people, he hath redeemed Jerusalem. The Lord hath made bare his holy arm in the eyes of all the nations; and all the ends of the earth shall see the salvation of God." (*The Book of Mormon*, 3 Nephi 16:13-

20 emphasis added.)

That happens to be Jesus Christ, after his resurrection, speaking to his "other sheep", the Nephites, (*The Holy Bible*, John 10:16; *The Book of Mormon*, 3 Nephi 15:11-14)

We are those Gentiles the Lord now commands to repent and RETURN unto him. If we repent and return unto him, we will be his people and he will be our God. This scripture becomes a Voice of Warning the Lord said he would give us. (*Doctrine & Covenants* 38:41)

Our inspired Constitution has been mauled and battered and is hanging as by a single thread. The Lord asks us to restore and preserve it, and anything the Lord asks us to do he will enable us to accomplish (*The Book of Mormon*, I Nephi 3:7)

Let's do it!

GOD BLESS AMERICA!

CHAPTER EIGHT – THE DEEP SOUTH

One fourth of my roots are out of the Deep South – out of Alabama and Mississippi in 1844 and out of North and South Carolina one generation earlier.

When my great great grandfather, Joseph Lazerus Matthews, and all his family were baptized into The Church of Jesus Christ of Latter-day Saints in Noxubee County, Mississippi in June of 1844, they owned a large plantation there and were very wealthy. When my great great grandfather John Daniel Holladay, Sr. and all his family were baptized into The Church of Jesus Christ of Latter-day Saints in Marion County, Alabama in the same month and year, they also were very wealthy and owned a large plantation there.

In the same month of June 1844, at Carthage, Illinois, Joseph and Hyrum Smith were killed and John Taylor was severely wounded by a mob with painted faces.

When they learned of the assassination of Joseph and Hyrum, the Matthews and Holladay families and other Latter-day Saints in Mississippi and Alabama requested instructions from the Quorum of the Twelve Apostles of the Church in Nauvoo, Illinois. They were told to free their slaves, sell their plantations, and prepare their families to go west and north into the Rocky Mountains with the rest of the Saints. They did so.

When the Holladays were baptized, fifty of their slaves were baptized at the same time, which leads me to believe they were not unkind or cruel taskmasters.

The Lord had said earlier, "Therefore, it is not right that any man should be in bondage one to another. And for this purpose have I established the Constitution of this land, by the hands of wise men whom I raised up unto this very purpose, and redeemed the land by the shedding of blood." (*Doctrine & Covenants* 101:79-80)

We sometimes hear criticism of our Constitution because it did not fully resolve and dispose of the problem of slavery once and for all. Dr. W. Cleon Skousen, however, assures us that the Founding Fathers had agreed that by a specified date all states were to pass a law pronouncing that anyone born in that state after that date would be a free citizen of that state and of the nation. Had that been carried out, slavery would have expired in one generation and that would have avoided the Civil War, or the War between the States, and the problems it caused. "It is not right that any man should be in bondage one to another." (*Doctrine & Covenants* 101:79)

Well, that would do away with slavery. However, the implementation of that decree took a little longer and turned out to be much more painful. That made the preaching of the restored gospel in the Deep South in those days very difficult. Some, however, did accept it, as did my own great great grandparents, who were willing to make whatever sacrifice might be required for the restored Church of Jesus Christ.

It may be well to note also, that the anti-slavery position of the Church contributed much to the opposition to the Church when the

Latter-day Saints were attempting to establish themselves in Missouri in the 1830's. That was a time of great competition between the so-called slave states and the "free" states, and many were striving diligently to make Missouri a slave state.

Another problem for the Latter-day Saints then, and sometimes even now, was the fact that other churches had a paid and professional ministry while the Latter-day Saints did not. Many of those ministers then, and also now, were as pleased and even proud, of their profession, as they would have been if they had been outstanding and successful school teachers, or directors or attendants in marriage counseling, or family relations counseling, or in financial counseling, or any other social service work. They, and you, and everyone else will certainly be rewarded in heaven for all the good they have done.

GOD BLESS AMERICA!

CHAPTER NINE – THE BIBLE BELT

I have always felt great love for the South, not only because that is where one fourth of all my roots are from, but also because of their religious and political stability, and the stability they give our nation.

Such faith and religious fervor do they have, that throughout our whole nation the entire region of the South is known collectively as our great "Bible Belt." They are particularly outstanding in their support of traditional families and family values. May our Father in Heaven richly bless them for it, and I know that He will.

When the Southern Baptists decided to hold their annual convention in Salt Lake City, several years ago, many of their leaders met with several members of the Council of the Twelve Apostles of The Church of Jesus Christ of Latter-day Saints for preliminary exchanges of ideas. At that time, Elder Neal A. Maxwell of the Council of the Twelve, remarked: "I propose that we begin by noting and accepting the fact that we are different. Instead of wasting our time arguing over what we <u>don't</u> agree on, let us pick some of the things we <u>do</u> agree on, such as traditional families, and discuss what we can do unitedly to improve things."

Could we suggest the same thing here? Let us work together to clean up Congress, and the Supreme Court, and all the rest of our government, from top to bottom, and surely our Father in Heaven will enable us to restore and strengthen our Constitution, which will bless our whole nation and everyone in it.

A story: A faithful Christian gentleman was sitting on his front porch when he noticed the waters were rising rapidly and his home was now surrounded by water on all sides. As he continued to observe, he noted the water was rising even much faster than he had at first thought. Soon the water was about to rise over the top of his porch. Just then, two men went by in a boat, and called to him, inviting to take him to safety, but he replied, "No thanks, the Lord will save me!"

A little later, as he was looking at the flood from an upstairs window, two other men went by in a boat and also offered to take him to safety, but he responded, "No, thanks, the Lord will save me."

But the flood waters got higher and higher, and finally he was observing them from his roof. About that time two more men went by in a helicopter overhead, and they called down to offer to take him to safety, but he responded, "No thanks, the Lord will save me."

A little later, in heaven, as he was talking with the Lord, he said, "You really let me down! I had such complete faith that you would save me!" The Lord said, "Let you down? I sent you two boats and a helicopter and you refused to get in!"

If we are going to be saved in this flood, maybe we are going to have to all cooperate, and not refuse to get in the boat just because the driver doesn't happen to belong to our particular parish or synagogue!

We need to elect leaders who are wise, good, (men of integrity), and honest (neither thieves nor liars). "When the righteous are in authority, the people rejoice, but when the wicked bear rule, the people mourn." (Proverbs 29:2)

Who determines who are "in authority"? The Voters. Who are the Voters? You, I, and thousands of others who haven't made it to the polls yet. Let us help them find their way. Teach them to use the Voters' Guide put out by the Christian Coalition that shows how Senators and Congressmen have voted on measures of concern to us. Also, teach them to pray for inspiration in choosing the *best* candidates.

One Southern Senator said, "To expect Congress to clean up Congress is like expecting a hog to butcher itself. We (the voters) could help them!

GOD BLESS AMERICA!

CHAPTER TEN – WHAT ELSE NEEDS TO BE FIXED?

About two or three years ago I received a letter in the mail urging me to sign a protest against action taken by the IRS in canceling the tax exempt status of a Protestant Church in New Jersey. A speaker had been permitted to speak there against Homosexuality. The minister considered that a moral issue. The IRS said, "Homosexuality is now a *political* matter."

The first amendment states: "Congress shall make no law abridging the freedom of Speech, or of the Press." If Congress cannot do that, where does the IRS get *their* authority to do it? Where in the Constitution does it say, "This applies to everybody but Churches?" If there is anyone in the whole nation that should *never* have their freedom of speech abridged it ought to be Churches, even in matters of politics! Of course, that problem would be resolved with the abolishment of the whole IRS when our monetary system is constitutionalized as recommended in chapter two.

A few years ago, a renter paid me a check, which was promptly deposited in the bank. I proceeded to write checks and pay bills. When notices of fees, charged for overdrafts, came in I learned the renter's check had also bounced. I contacted the renter to protest. He told me *the IRS had seized his whole bank account without even telling him,* to say nothing of waiting until he had been declared guilty in a court of law.

In a constitutional republic, can't we all play ball on the same level court without having special and unconstitutional privileges given to the IRS and denied to our citizens, without even a trial in a court of law? The next problem is that under our constitution the accused *is to be presumed innocent until he has been proven guilty in a court of law. Under the IRS, the accused is presumed guilty until* **HE** *can prove himself innocent.*

The next IRS problem is one of *organization*. The Founding Fathers set up our national government with *three separate departments* – Legislative, Executive, and Judicial. The IRS appears to embody all three. They make the laws and Congress approves them, they do the enforcing, and finally they hold their own hearing as a Judiciary in the matter. Of course, all this will also be corrected with the abolishment of the IRS when our tax and monetary programs are constitutionalized, as herein recommended.

There are also other things to be fixed, but when we get even this many handled, it will be a real blessing!

GOD BLESS AMERICA!

CHAPTER ELEVEN – ZION

Predicting the latter-day Restoration, the Apostle Peter declared: "Repent ye therefore, and be converted, that your sins may be blotted out, when the times of refreshing shall come from the presence of the Lord;

"And he shall send Jesus Christ, which before was preached unto you: Whom the heaven must receive until the times of restitution of all things, which God hath spoken by the mouth of all his holy prophets since the world began" (*The Holy Bible*, Acts 3:19-21)

Does that mean this restitution was spoken of by all of God's holy prophets since the world began? Or does it mean the restitution itself will restore everything God has ever spoken by the mouth of all his holy prophets since the world began? In either case that will be quite a restitution or restoring indeed!

One of the things to be restored, obviously, is the book of Enoch, and the great things revealed therein concerning his city, which was named Zion, which we are told means, "the pure in heart" (*Doctrine and Covenants* 97:21)

One of the assignments of the Lord's people in our day will be to establish another City of Zion, which will be called the New Jerusalem, patterned after the City of Enoch. What were the characteristics of the City of Enoch?

"And the Lord called His people Zion because they were *of one heart* [desire] and one mind [they thought alike] and dwelt in Righteousness [no Sin among them], and there was *no poor among them.*" (*Pearl of Great Price,* Moses 7:18)

It does not say there were no wealthy among them, but because they lived the United Order there were *no poor among them* – They were *all rich.* That is one thing we have to restore. That is the main reason the Lord gave us the Constitution. The Constitution is the law of *Financial Liberty.* The Lord never intended to set up a Government that would plunder His people and seize their property to give to someone else. That was a 1934 innovation, as was also the philosophy of the Government buying prosperity by always running in debt, so that is another constitutional apostasy that will need to be corrected.

"We believe that Governments were instituted by God for the benefit of man; and that He holds men accountable for their acts in relation to them, both *in making laws and administering them,* for the good and safety of society.

"We believe that no government can exist in peace except such laws are framed and held inviolate as will secure to each individual the *free exercise of conscience, the right and control of property,* and the protection of life." (*Doctrine & Covenants* 134:1-2)

Nearly everything in our Society today operates on the basis of *greed.* From the poor, greedily encouraging the government to seize other people's property so they can share in the plunder of the wealth, to the wealthy raising prices so high the needy can't even meet their basic needs of food, clothing, and shelter.

But that is not the Lord's program and we'd better conquer greed and do it the Lord's way. That is why he gave us our Constitution. **So, let's do it!**

GOD BLESS AMERICA!

CHAPTER TWELVE – PROSPERITY

The good Lord never intended for His people to be so poverty-stricken they can not even have a roof over their head. That was not the Lord's program and that is not the way our God-given Constitution set it up.

We just read that in the city of Enoch, living God-given laws, there were *no poor among them*. (*Pearl of Great Price*, Moses 7:18) If there were no poor among them, *they must have had prosperity*. That is the Lord's program and that is our Constitution's program. The Constitution was set up *to promote the General Welfare* and under that program, as directed by our Constitution, *Congress was to create and control our money.*

That is the way the Lord gave it. However, in 1912 and 1913 President Woodrow Wilson and our millionaire Senator Allrich persuaded Congress to abdicate their Constitutional responsibility and *turn it over to the Banks, which they did in the Federal Reserve Act in 1913, making this consortium of private banks the Central Bank of our Nation.*

Thomas Jefferson apparently foresaw this Constitutional apostasy for he wrote: "If the American people ever allow private banks to control the issue of their money, first by inflation and then by deflation, the banks and corporations that will grow up around them, will deprive their people of their property until their children will wake up *homeless* on the Continent their Fathers conquered."

That is where we stand today. *Let us restore our Constitution and regain our prosperity.* As discussed in an earlier chapter, Federal Reserve Chairman, Alan Greenspan recently raised interest rates to "cool" the economy. That would reduce our money, he explained, and thereby avoid inflation, since, he explains, "Inflation is caused by too much money chasing too few goods".

Solution? Simple. Double our money and quadruple the production of our goods which we can do when we abolish the Federal Reserve Board and the IRS and taxes and have Congress create our money instead of the banks and we can all invest in plants and businesses all over the land instead of spending half of all we earn for taxes.

Would you like prosperity in our Nation? Restore the Constitution and we will have it!

GOD BLESS AMERICA!

CHAPTER THIRTEEN – TO PROMOTE THE GENERAL WELFARE

Tax reforms advocated by Jack Kemp and others are exactly right. Now let us go a step further and correct the whole problem. The Constitution says, "*Congress* shall have power to coin money (and) regulate the value thereof." (Article I, Section 8, Clause 8).

Some say they do not trust Congress. Then let us elect men we *can* trust.

When Congress creates our money instead of the banks, we can abolish taxes *and* the IRS *and* the Federal Reserve. The Government will already *have* the money and will not *need* to *collect it.*

That money would then be put into circulation through legitimate expenses of government. It would also be put into circulation by *loans* to the banks, *at interest.* That interest would pay part of the cost of the government as taxes do now. Moreover, the money with which to *pay* the interest would also be *created.* We would not have an impossible situation, as we do now, with the *banks* creating the money *out of nothing* and putting it into circulation as a *loan* to the government, which means the *taxpayer,* but without any money being created with which to *pay* the interest.

No wonder wives feel they have to go to work just to make ends meet. Since no interest-free money exists with which to *pay* the *interest* on the money created by the bank and put into circulation *as a loan*, the banks will continue to repossess our farms, our homes, and everything else. *Eventually the government will own nothing, the people will own nothing, and the banks will own everything.* That is the only possible eventual outcome of our present impossible all-debt monetary system. We would do better to back off and correct this serious error before nobody owns his own home, as Thomas Jefferson predicted.

In his book "Debt Virus", Dr. Jacques S. Jaikaran, M. D. points out that *this will occur in about the year 2012, if everything continues as it is now going and without correction.* A mathematical error never should have been made in the first place. It could and should be corrected now before it all comes down around our ears. According to the present trend, if this serious error is permitted to continue, *by about the year 2012, the yearly interest alone on our national debt will exceed all money in circulation, says Dr. Jaikaran.*

The Lord said we are to elect men who are *wise, honest, and good* (men of integrity). When we do that, we will be able to trust them. When we have that kind of leaders, we will restore our constitution, preserve it, and follow it.

"And when we obtain any blessing from God it is by obedience to that law upon which it is predicated." (Doctrine &

Covenants 130:21)

That is the way it is in science, in making an electric motor, and in flying to the moon. It is also the way it is in having peace and harmony in our homes and communities. That is the way it will be when we restore our constitution and comprehend that, our Father in Heaven is the one who inspired it.

They wrote it to promote the "*GENERAL* WELFARE", not just the *specific* welfare of a few great and powerful special interests.

GOD BLESS AMERICA!

CHAPTER FOURTEEN – LET'S RESTORE IT!

A photocopy of a newspaper article entitled "The National Debt" from the newspaper "The News," Lynchburg, Virginia, of Saturday. March 26, 1977, states: "In 1901 the National Debt of the U. S. was less than 1 billion dollars. It remained less than 1 billion dollars until we got into World War I. Then it jumped to 25 billion dollars."

From 1918 to 1941, it increased from 25 billion dollars to 49 billion dollars. From 1942 to 1952, it rose to 265 billion dollars. In 1962, it was 303 billion dollars; in 1970 it was 383 billion dollars; by 1976, it was 631 billion dollars; and by March 26, 1977, it reached 727 billion dollars, having nearly doubled in the last eight years. The article continues "If the present trend continues *we can expect the national debt to nearly double again within the next six to eight years...eventually, the government will own nothing, the people will own nothing, the banks will own everything.*"

In his book, "Billions for the Bankers, Debts for the People," Pastor Sheldon Emery of Sand Point, Idaho, points out that throughout history nations have been conquered by the use of one or more of three methods

1. War

2. Religion

3. Economic conquests, (where people are placed under "tribute"

without physical force or coercion so the victims do not realize they have been conquered.)

In 1900 the average American paid few taxes and had little debt, now, debts and taxes consume more than half of what is earned.

The Restoration Prophet Joseph Smith predicted our Constitution would become so battered that eventually it would hang "as by a single thread."

He is quoted as having said, that at that critical point "The Elders of this church will step forth and save it." At least let us hope they will. Otherwise, things are looking a little doubtful.

Well, this is the time of Restoration. Let us step forth now and save our Constitution and our Constitution will most surely save us!

GOD BLESS AMERICA!

CHAPTER FIFTEEN – THE PEOPLE MOURN

One night as I was taking the Massachusetts Av. Exit from Highway 94, in Lemon Grove, California, a man was standing at the side of the road, at the traffic light, holding a sign which said, "Homeless Vet. Please Help. God Bless." Not having any bills in my wallet, I just reached into my pocket and handed him a handful of coins, and he even appreciated that.

Driving home, I remembered the scripture in the Bible that says, "When the righteous are in authority, the people rejoice, but when the wicked rule, the people mourn." As homes become harder and harder to get, and even the price of food gets higher and higher, I couldn't help wondering if having no roof over your head and no food in your stomach might not cause a lot of people nowadays to "mourn." It is not causing them to do much "rejoicing", I am sure.

Our politicians, of course, keep reassuring us that we have no inflation. Then why does it now cost from ten to twenty times as much to buy or build a house as it did thirty or forty years ago? And why do so many mothers now feel that they are compelled to go to work just to make ends meet? *Is that causing a little mourning?* And what about the *social problems* that become the natural consequences of mothers leaving their children to go to work; Are those causing a little mourning also?

Jeremiah was calling the rebellious ancient Israelites to repentance. They were not only worshipping idols, but were even offering up their children as sacrifices to them by burning them in the fire. "How grotesque!" We exclaim. But what of the millions of innocent defenseless babies in our own land killed every year in a manner hardly less grotesque than in ancient Judah. As the baby is in the process of birth, a hole is punched in his head and his brains are sucked out with a vacuum cleaner.

How can we correct all that so we can rejoice instead of mourn? By repenting and returning to the God who created us. That is the God of the Holy Bible, all current mocking to the contrary notwithstanding. When we become a moral and righteous citizenry, we will elect moral and righteous leaders, and "When the righteous are in authority, the people will rejoice! They will indeed!

GOD BLESS AMERICA!

CHAPTER SIXTEEN – A LEVEL PLAYING FIELD

Before the Great Depression of 1929 my father-in-law, John William Jones, owned a lumber yard, a planing mill, an apartment house and a home in Ogden, Utah, and was prosperous. He was a builder and a number of people owed him money and paid him regularly. The banks closed and people were unable to draw out their money to make payments on their financial obligations. Before it was all over with he had lost his business, his lumber yard, his apartment house, his income, and his home and moved to California with five hundred dollars in his pocket to try to earn a living there selling Maytag washing machines.

He couldn't compel others to pay *him*, but the *banks could compel him to pay them*, even if they had to move him and his family into the street, so they could repossess his home and all else he owned, which they did.

If we are going to play ball, why don't we all play ball on the same court, and why isn't the field level? Why don't we all play by the same rules?

My last year in high school I lived with my Aunt Mary Merrell's family in Naples, Utah, three miles southeast of Vernal. About March of that year 1933, she received a letter from her friendly banker:

Dear Mrs. Merrell:

Inasmuch as you have not been making mortgage payments on the eight hundred dollars you owe us, please have your property vacated by _____ (date) so we can repossess it.

Sincerely yours,

Your friendly banker.

She moved out and they moved in. To satisfy her debt of eight hundred dollars they seized her whole farm, and her home and everything in them or on them. She never even received a note of thanks, nor a dime of change.

Why not? They were not required to send it. That is the law. The field all slopes in the same direction, always in the favor of the banks. That is just the way it is.

I'm still waiting for the bank to tell me what I can foreclose on to get back the $19.45 of mine they held in deposit when they said they went broke early in the depression.

With the IRS, it is even worse. If you owe them anything, they are threatening to send you to prison, but if you want to report a loss they will let you claim it at about 3% per year for the next thirty years or so. Why can't we all play on the same level field and by the same rules?

When Congress passes laws why don't they apply to everyone the same? I used to wonder why the biggest building in every city is always owned by the banks. I used to wonder how they could do that with loans out at 8% interest.

Finally, the explanation was given. Present laws permit banks to loan out at interest up to ten times as much money as they actually own. So that makes the interest they receive to be 80% instead of 8%.

What do you think would happen to you if *you* started loaning out at interest ten times as much money as you actually own? Maybe we all ought to be playing by the same rules, and on the same court, and maybe it ought to be level.

GOD BLESS AMERICA!

CHAPTER SEVENTEEN – ENOUGH AND TO SPARE

We have spoken of the Lord's law of sharing. Even to the extent we are now obeying this law, what a blessing it is to mankind, and especially to the needy among us.

We see all around us "thrift stores" managed by churches and other charitable institutions. To them we may contribute articles of clothing or anything else we no longer need. To these thrift stores the needy and others as well, may go to buy clothing and other necessities at a price they can afford. In these institutions the aged, the infirm, and the handicapped have an opportunity to work to whatever degree they are able, in order to maintain their honor and dignity and self-reliance. What a blessing indeed.

Goods produced and assembled for the relief of the needy are often used also for the relief of victims of floods, fire, earthquakes, or other disaster, and what a blessing they are there also! At times well-meaning people have suggested having the government take over this whole business of relief of the needy. They can pass laws and collect taxes and seize properties whether anyone wants to contribute or not! That, of course, is precisely the problem. That procedure violates the Lord's law of "free agency", and therefore debases rather than blesses. We are blessed only by and for what we *voluntarily* and *cheerfully* give.

"Every man according as he purposeth in his heart, so let him give, not grudgingly, or of necessity: for God loveth a *cheerful* giver." (2 Corinthians 9:6-7, emphasis added)

By latter-day revelation, as part of the promised Restoration, the Lord has had some rather interesting things to say about all this:

I, the Lord, stretched out the heavens, and built the earth, my very handiwork, and all things therein are mine.

But it must needs be done in mine own way; and behold this is the way that I, the Lord, have decreed to provide for my saints, that the poor shall be exalted, in that the rich are made low.

For the earth is full, and there is enough and to spare; yea, I prepared all things, and have given unto the children of men to be agents unto themselves." (Doctrine & Covenants 104:14-17)

"The poor shall be exalted, in that the rich are made low." How is that to be done? By the tax collector, perhaps, or the government seizing properties? No, indeed, that is not the Lord's way. Where the rich are taught the true principles of the Lord's gospel and are inspired to obey them, the poor will be exalted by having a bed to sleep in and a roof over their head, and food to eat, and work to do in order to *earn* them.

Yes, the rich will be "made low", but only in the sense that they have cheerfully and voluntarily given of their goods to bless the lives of others. However, while they may be "made low" in that sense, in a broader sense they too will be "exalted" by the Lord.

The revelation concerning Enoch and his city says:

"The Lord called his people Zion, because they were of one heart and one mind, and dwelt in righteousness, and there was no poor among them." (*Pearl of Great Price*, Moses 7:13-18)

So great was the faith of Enoch, that he led the people of God. Their enemies came to battle against them. Enoch spake the word of the Lord, and the earth trembled, and the mountains fled, even according to his command. The rivers of water were turned out of their course. The roar of the lions was heard out of the wilderness; and all nations feared greatly, so powerful was the word of Enoch, and so great was the power of the language which God had given him.

That is what happened then and that is what has to happen again in our day, and that is why the Lord gave the revelation previously referred to *which sets forth this solemn warning*:

"Therefore, if any man shall take of the abundance which I have made, and *impart not his portion, according to the law of my gospel, unto the poor and the needy, he shall, with the wicked, lift up his eyes in hell, being in torment.*" (Doctrine & Covenants 104:18, emphasis added)

It sounds like the Lord takes that rather seriously, does it not. He obviously expects us to do likewise! "God loveth a cheerful giver!" "For the earth is full and there is enough and to spare!"

GOD BLESS AMERICA!

CHAPTER EIGHTEEN – BLESSED IS THE NATION

As we learn to work together as God-fearing Christians, Arabs, and Jews, and others, for the advancement of righteousness in the earth we will bless the lives of all of our Father in Heaven's children all over the earth. "Blessed is the Nation whose God is the Lord!" (Psalms 13:12) What a delight that will be! "When the righteous are in authority, the people rejoice, but when the wicked bear rule, the people mourn." (Proverbs 29:2)

What makes us mourn? Taxes, so much crime we need a good dog, a gun, or iron bars on our windows, or move to a "gated community"? Would it be widespread homelessness, depression, and devaluation of our money, or maybe all of the above? We have no inflation, our politicians assure us. We never had it so good! Then why does it now cost from ten to twenty times as much to buy or build a house to live in as it did fifty years ago? Why do so many women feel compelled to leave their children to go to work outside the home, to help earn enough money to even survive?

As previously noted, Thomas Jefferson predicted: "If the American people ever allow private banks to control the issue of their money, first by inflation and then by deflation, the banks and corporations that will grow up around them, will deprive the people of their property until their children will wake up homeless on the continent their fathers conquered."

The issuance of our money has been controlled by private banks through nearly all of our existence as a nation, and totally since the establishment of the Federal Reserve Bank in 1913. Are we seeing any of the results Jefferson predicted? Jefferson continued: "The issuing power of money should be taken from the banks and restored to Congress and the people to whom it belongs. The banking institutions having the issuing power of money, are more dangerous to liberty than standing armies." (Dwinell, Olive C., The Story of Our Money, quoted in Jaikaran, Jacques S., M.D., "Debt Virus, A Compelling Solution to the World's Debt Problems." P. 7)

A newspaper article quoted earlier in chapter fourteen entitled "The National Debt" in the newspaper "The News", at Lynchburg, Virginia, on Saturday March 26, 1977, traced our National Debt from 1901 to 1977. It was less than one billion dollars in 1901, $25 billion at the close of World War I and $49 billion on the eve of World War II, it was $72 billion in 1941, $265 billion in 1952 and $303 billion in 1962. It was $383 billion in 1970, $631 billion in 1976, and estimated to reach $727 billion by the end of 1977 and over $800 billion in 1978, "having nearly doubled in the past eight years." The article continues: "If the present trend continues… we can expect the national debt to nearly double again within the next six to eight years…. *Eventually the government will own nothing, the people will own nothing, (and) the banks will own everything.*"

Are we seeing anything like that? How many people now own their own home, or even their own automobile? If all the so-called "owners" really own is the privilege of making payments on them, who is really the "owner"?

Dr. Jacques S. Jaikaran, M. D., wrote a book entitled "Debt virus, A Compelling Solution to the World's Debt Problems." The author, a medical doctor, M.D. spent eight years researching the monetary systems all over the earth, nearly all of which are all-debt money systems, like our own. He writes:

When money is created as a debt is the interest charged likewise created? The answer is no. That is the crux of the problem... This flaw dooms our present monetary system to failure... It is speeding our day of judgment unless entirely new corrective measures are taken". (p. 7). "The disease is our debt-dominant money system, which has a built-in mathematical error. Correct this error and cure the disease. The symptoms will disappear. (p. 70)

On page 96, Jaikaran quotes Abraham Lincoln as saying, after the passage of the National Banking Act in 1863, "I see in the near future a crisis approaching that unnerves me and causes me to tremble for the safety of my country. Corporations have been enthroned. An era of corruption in high places will follow. The money power of the country will endeavor to prolong its reign by working upon the prejudices of the people until the wealth is aggregated in a few hands and the Republic is destroyed." (What happened to that "*General* Welfare?") Dr Jaikaran continues:

We have nationalized a system of economic oppression that is equally as damnable as the Lincoln era of chattel slavery." ... "Whenever the private banks create money out of thin air as debt and loan this money to the government, sooner or later such an act will lead to escalating government debt, high interest rates, high taxes, and political and economic instability. (p.99)

The Federal Reserve System was supposed to avoid financial panics, recessions, and economic depressions and to stabilize the purchasing power of our currency. Yet, we suffered the most devastating depression in our history in 1929, a mere sixteen years after its establishment. Additionally, a 1990-dollar is now worth no more than six cents compared with the 1900-dollar."... " The money creators, by withholding credit, can cause an economic depression at will. It was the gradual contraction of the money supply that eventually led to the recession of 1920-21. The Great Depression of 1929 was similarly engineered. (p. 109)

Citizens really ought to read the whole book, and maybe a few more books as well, to know what is really going on. When I first became aware of the fact that under the present system, the Federal Reserve Bank creates our money out of thin air and then gives it to the federal government as a *loan*, for the tax-payers to have to pay interest on, I said to myself *"That is the stupidest thing I ever heard of! Why doesn't the government create its own money, and loan it to the banks and let the banks pay interest on it and use the interest to pay the legitimate constitutional expenses of government?"*

That is exactly what this author recommends as the only effective cure of our present disease of Debt Virus, which will otherwise destroy us.

1. Central banks not owned by the government should be dissolved, and private banks will then be *under a 100 percent reserve requirement.*

2. Banks thus charted and organized could loan only what they

have, or what they can borrow, *but would be forbidden from creating money.*

3. It is legally the government's business, through its national Treasury, to print, create, and provide coins, paper, or checkbook money for the national economy;

4. The national Treasury, on orders of Congress, would create money and purchase interest-bearing bonds from the borrowing banks;

5. The interest rates charged on all treasury loans would be determined by the treasury's computer, which could be programmed *to maintain the flow of treasury revenues in close balance with the flow of treasury expenditures;*

6. Money would be added to the economy through debt-free government expenditures and through loans made by the treasury mainly to banks or, in certain cases, directly to industry;

7. Banks would be just like any other business enterprise. *They would not create money nor would they receive any free raw material like reserves.* The principal source of their lending funds would *be the savings of the people.* If banks did need more money, they could borrow from the national treasury.

8. *Income taxes and most other taxes would be abolished.* Legitimate constitutional expenses of the government would be paid for by check from the national Treasury, thus injecting that money into the economy of the nation.

9. The Federal Reserve System and the Internal Revenue Service would both be abolished.

This whole recommendation, of course, is exactly what the Constitution says was supposed to be done in the first place. Article 1,

Section 8, Close 5, of the Constitution of the United States says, *"Congress shall have power to coin (print) our money and regulate the value thereof."*

In over 200 years Congress never did get around to filling this assignment by the Constitution, which caused endless confusion, as many different state banks and private banks were printing their own money. And finally, in 1913, in the passing of the Federal Reserve Act, they turned the whole matter over to the banks to handle, which some people have felt was about as smart as assigning the fox to guard the henhouse.

Our national debt is now at roughly six trillion dollars. If present trends continue, in our all-debt money system, this author points out that by about the year 2012 "the annual interest alone on the public debt will be equal to or greater than all the money in circulation. At this time, the bubble will burst, and there will occur a total financial collapse in the United States." (p. 105)

Well, that is *his* weather report on the approaching storm. We can do nothing and just let the storm hit, or *we can decide to re-instate the Constitution and do it like the Constitution says it is supposed to be done.*

All that brings us back to the point of beginning. The Bible says, "Blessed is the nation whose God is the Lord." The founders of this nation, and its Constitution, were God-fearing, Bible-reading, and Bible-believing men. They studied the Bible, especially the Book of Deuteronomy, for their inspiration for setting up our government and our Constitution. This nation was set up, initially, as a nation whose "God is the Lord."

And by the inspiration of the Lord, the Constitution was framed to make sure we stayed that way, and to "form a more perfect Union, establish Justice, insure domestic Tranquility, provide for the common defense, promote the general Welfare, and secure the Blessings of Liberty to ourselves and our Posterity."

I once saw a sign in the back window of a car in front of me. It said: "They took prayer out of our schools; They took the Bible out of our schools; They took God out of our schools; and now our prisons are full!" That reminded me of a video I had just seen at the recommendation of our son, Dr. Maynard Robert Olsen, M.D., entitled America's Godly Heritage, produced by David Barton, Wall Builders, P.O. Box 397, Aledo, TX 76008.

In this video, David Barton points out that the founding fathers who drew up the Constitution and founded this nation were God-fearing Bible-reading Bible-believing Christians. They set this nation up very definitely to be a Christian nation. During the first century and a half of our existence, the Supreme Court ruled several times that this nation is indeed a Christian nation.

Barton shows that in the Supreme Court rulings of 1962, banning prayer, and the Bible, and God, from our public schools, the Supreme Court was exceeding its Constitutional functions, and was usurping the legislative powers of Congress in the ruling it issued. He presents statistics, including bar charts showing how uncanny it is that the year 1962 is the exact breaking point where everything bad in the United States suddenly became much worse and everything good suddenly plummeted.

The Lord raised up the Reformers to do the great work of Reformation that had to be done in preparation for the Restoration that was to follow. The Reformers translated the Bible into the languages of the common man, and organized societies and churches to promote the reading and understanding of the Bible. The Lord then raised up God-fearing men who established this great nation with its inspired Constitution and its laws of liberty and freedom, which was the only nation on the face of the whole earth where he could restore his Church and his Gospel at the time they were restored. By latter-day revelation, the Lord has said that he raised up the men who drew up the Constitution of this nation and inspired them to produce it. It is therefore our civic responsibility to preserve and sustain it. To Latter-day Saints that is the mind and will of the Lord. To everyone else it is proposed as a good idea quite capable of standing on its own merits.

In any case, it should be quite apparent that if the Constitution is going to be sustained, it will be we citizens who are going to have to sustain it! How do we do that? We need to repent of our own sins and obey the Ten Commandments. Men and women without integrity do not elect officials who have it! The bible says, *"He that ruleth over men must be just, ruling in the fear of God!"* (2 Samuel 23:3, emphasis added)

What is all this prattle about our leaders not having to be men of integrity? That is not what the Bible says! What they forget is what the Bible *does* say: *"When the righteous are in authority; the people rejoice, but when the wicked bear rule, the people mourn"*. (Proverbs 29:2)

Who control that? You and I do, the VOTERS. So, we had better get out and VOTE, and get others to do likewise. Study the issues, study the candidates, pray about them, and then let your conscience be your guide. If we are sincere and pray in faith, we will get some help from our Heavenly Father and get this thing turned around before we go over the cliff. What else do we find in the Bible that has any bearing on this subject? "To him that knoweth to do good, and doeth it not, to him it is sin." (James 4:17)

A story previously told: A faithful Christian gentleman was sitting on his front porch when he noticed the waters were rising rapidly and his home was now surrounded by water on all sides. As he continued to observe, he noted the water was rising even much faster than he had at first thought. Soon the water was about to rise over the top of his porch. Just then, two men went by in a boat, and called to him, inviting to take him to safety, but he replied, "No thanks, the Lord will save me!"

A little later, as he was looking at the flood from an upstairs window, two other men went by in a boat and also offered to take him to safety, but he responded, 'No thanks, the Lord will save me.' "But the flood waters got higher and higher, and finally he was observing them from his roof. About that time two more men went by in a helicopter overhead, and they called down to offer to take him to safety, but he responded, 'No thanks, the Lord will save me.'

A little later, in heaven, as he was talking with the Lord, he said, "You really let me down! And I had such complete faith that you would save me!" The Lord said, "Let you down? I sent you two boats and a helicopter and you refused to get in!"

If we are going to be saved in this flood, maybe we are going to have to all cooperate, and not refuse to get in the boat just because the driver doesn't happen to belong to our particular parish or synagogue!"

Blessed is the nation whose God is the Lord!

GOD BLESS AMERICA!

CHAPTER NINETEEN – PRIORITIES

What in the world were the Supreme Court thinking of when they decided to legalize abortions, killing millions of innocent defenseless American babies before they were even born, or in the very process of birth?

What was the Supreme Court thinking of in 1962 when they decided to re-write the Compulsory Education Law, instead of simply declaring it, null and void and sending it back to Congress and the States to write a new one?

What in the world is the Supreme Court thinking of now when it permits the IRS, Congress, or even the President to violate the Constitution by abridging the freedom of speech or of the press to prevent churches or anyone else from speaking freely on political matters? (First Amendment)

Obviously, the first need of all is to pass a proposed Judicial and Supreme Court Amendment to serve as a "check and balance" on the Supreme Court and federal judges to prevent them from violating the very Constitution, they have taken an oath to sustain and preserve. Where was the Supreme Court when they permitted Congress and the President to have the banks create and control our money (through the Federal Reserve Act of 1913), instead of Congress creating and controlling our money, as the Constitution directs?

It would appear that our second priority should be to repeal the Federal Reserve Act and the Federal Income Tax, abolish the IRS and Federal Reserve, and instruct Congress and the President to create and control our money as President Abraham Lincoln did during the Civil War. The banks should be forbidden to loan out at interest more money than they have in deposit, and the whole monetary program should be revised. The abolishment of taxes and restructuring of the complete monetary system would appear to be the next priority.

When the Compulsory Education laws are rewritten, provisions should be made for parents to put children in schools of their own choice, funded by the same dollars "public" schools receive, and the Supreme Court's eviction of God, the Bible, prayer, and the Ten Commandments should be ordered terminated by Congress and the President, under the new Supreme Court amendment. The next priority would be to conduct a thorough debate concerning the repeal of the 17th Amendment. If repealed, the senators would again be appointed by their state and would serve to represent the interests of their state and prohibit the federal government from usurping powers not authorized by the Constitution.

Congress should reject Federal Reserve Chairman, Alan Greenspan's recommendation to "cool" our economy and reduce the quantity of money in circulation in order to avoid inflation, caused by "too much money chasing too few goods."

Instead, they should create more money, place more money in circulation, and double or treble that production of "goods" by every plant or business of every kind in our nation to discourage inflation by greatly increasing the quantity of goods in circulation, throughout all the land!

GOD BLESS AMERICA!

CHAPTER TWENTY – JUDGMENTS

In a latter-day revelation received at Kirtland Ohio on August 6, 1833, as part of the great Restoration foretold by Peter we read: "And now verily I say unto you concerning the laws of the land, it is my will that my people should observe to do all things whatsoever I command them.

*And that law of the land which is **constitutional**, supporting that principle of freedom in maintaining rights and privileges, **belongs to all mankind**, and is justifiable before me.*

*Therefore, I, the Lord, justify you and your brethren of my church, in befriending that law which is the **constitutional law of the land;***

And as pertaining to the law of man, whatsoever is more or less than this, cometh of evil." (Doctrine & Covenants 98:4-7)

Let's take another look and see what else we can learn about our Constitution from Latter-day Revelation received from God as part of the great Restoring promised by Peter (Act 3:19-21), and by the Prophet Daniel long before that, we might add (Daniel 2:44).

From a revelation received at Kirtland, Ohio on December 16, 1833:

Verily I say unto you, concerning your brethren who have been afflicted and persecuted, and cast out from the land of their inheritance, in Missouri. And again I say unto you, those who have been scattered by their enemies it is my will that they should continue to importune for redress, and redemption by the hand of those who are placed as rulers and are in authority over you –

According to the laws and constitution of the people, which I have suffered to be established, and should be maintained, for the rights and protection of all flesh, according to just and holy principles; That every man may act in doctrine and principle pertaining to futurity, according to the moral agency which I have given unto him, that every man may be accountable for his own sins in the day of judgment.

Therefore, it is not right that any man should be in bondage one to another. And for this purpose have I established the Constitution of this land, by the hands of wise men whom I raised up unto this very purpose and redeemed the land by the shedding of blood. (Doctrine & Covenants 101:1,76-80)

The Lord would not have permitted the persecution of the Saints in Missouri if they had been really worthy:

I, the Lord, have suffered the affliction to come upon them, wherewith they have been afflicted in consequence of their transgression; Yet I will own them, and they shall be mine in the day when I shall come to make up my jewels. Therefore, they must needs be chastened and tried, even as Abraham who was commanded to offer up his only son. For all those who will not endure chastening, but deny me, cannot be sanctified.

There were *jarrings*, and *contentions*, and *envyings*, and *strife*, and *lustful* and *covetous* desires among them, *therefore by these things they polluted their inheritances*

They were slow to hearken unto the voice of the Lord their God; therefore, the Lord their God is slow to hearken unto their prayers to answer them in the day of their trouble. In the day of their peace, they esteemed lightly my counsel; but in their trouble, of necessity they feel after me. Verily I say unto you, notwithstanding their sins, my bowels are filled with compassion towards them. I will not utterly cast them off; and in the day of wrath, I will remember mercy.

I have sworn and the decree hath gone forth by a former commandment which I have given unto you, that I would let fall the sword of mine indignation in behalf of my people; and even as I have said, it shall come to pass. [The U. S. Civil War, perhaps?]

Mine indignation is soon to be poured out without measure upon all nations; and this will I do *when the cup of their iniquity is full."* [World War I and World War II, perhaps?] (*Doctrine & Covenants* 101: 2-11, emphasis and brackets added)

It is my will that they should continue to importune for redress and redemption, *by the hands of those who are placed as rulers and are in authority over you –*

According to the laws and Constitution of the People, which I have suffered to be established, and should be maintained for the rights and protection of all flesh according to just and holy principles." (Doctrine & Covenants 101:76-77, emphasis added)

"Let them importune at the feet of the *judge*;

And if he heeds them not, let them importune at the feet of the *governor*;

And if the governor heed them not, let them importune at the feet of the *president*.

And if the President heed them not, then will the Lord come forth out of his hiding place and in his fury vex the nation." (Doctrine & Covenants 101: 86-89, emphasis added)

The President, Martin Van Buren, said, "Gentlemen, your cause is just, but I can do nothing for you. If I help you I will lose the vote of Missouri."

Interestingly enough he lost the vote of Missouri anyway.

The Governor of Missouri issued an executive order commanding all Latter-day Saints to leave the State or be executed, but it was repealed 150 years later.

The mobs got a few haystacks, mules, grain, and farms. The President lost the vote of Missouri. The Latter-day Saints were robbed, beaten, raped and murdered and finally they were driven en masse outside the bounds of the whole nation. *Fifteen years later, the Civil War drenched the whole land in blood.*

Maybe the Lord is paying closer attention to what is going on down here than some people think. Maybe this message really IS a "Voice of Warning" after all. (Doctrine & Covenants 38:41)

If you are looking for safety, obey the law of chastity, obey the Ten Commandments, and do not persecute the Lord's people or fight against the Twelve Apostles.

GOD BLESS AMERICA!

CHAPTER TWENTY-ONE – PROPOSED JUDICIAL AND SUPREME COURT CONSTITUTIONAL AMENDMENT

Many years ago, while still serving as a Special Agent of the United States Federal Bureau of Investigation (FBI), the Assistant Special Agent in Charge of our office said to me one day, "Every time the Supreme Court declares a different meaning to any phrase in the Constitution they have in effect revised it."

It appears that no one had any authority to stop them then, and no one has any authority to stop them now, though if something isn't done soon, they will not only have usurped the powers of the Congress, but even of the President as well.

Thomas Jefferson once said his greatest regret was that when the Founding Fathers placed checks and balances on the Congress (the presidential veto) and on the President (Congress could over-ride his veto), no checks or balances of any kind were placed on the Supreme Court. Nor have they ever been placed on Federal Judges. Both continue usurping powers not granted in the Constitution.

We are now two centuries overdue. That is the purpose of this book. It would appear that the only way to do it would be through passing now a Judicial Constitutional Amendment which would:

No. 1 – Forbid Federal Judges and the Supreme Court from

usurping legislation powers. *They have none.*

No. 2. – Require all Federal Judges and Supreme Court justices to be reconfirmed by the President and Congress every six years to continue to serve.

No. 3 – Authorize the President and Congress, with a two-thirds majority, to challenge and to veto any decision of the Supreme Court, or any Federal Judge, in any matter, past or present.

When anyone in our whole land is told when he can pray, and when he cannot, isn't that passing a *law*? In addition, isn't the making of laws *legislation*?

However, the Constitution says, "All legislataive powers herein granted shall be vested in a Congress of the United States, which shall consist of a Senate and House of Representatives." When a Federal Judge decides to rewrite the Pledge of Allegiance to eliminate the words "Under God," is he not in fact exercising powers he has never been given?

When another Federal Judge decides to seize a Ten Commandments monument to remove it from a State Supreme Court office, and decides to remove the State Supreme Court Chief Justice from office for having it there, whose power is he usurping to do that?

We need an amendment to prevent Federal Judges and Supreme Court Justices from usurping powers they do not really have, and we need to make sure the President and Congress remove them from office when they violate the constitution by such usurpations!

GOD BLESS AMERICA!

CHAPTER TWENTY-TWO – CANCER

Several years ago, a family named Jensen caused quite a stir in Utah. Their twelve-year-old son was sick and taken to the hospital for treatment. The doctors who attended him declared that in their opinion he had cancer, and recommended that he be treated with chemotherapy.

The patient did not want chemotherapy and his parents did not want him to have it. The doctors, however, were insistent and legal documents were drawn up to compel the parents to have their son given chemotherapy, whether they, or he, wanted it or not.

The parents thereupon took their twelve-year-old son and returned to Idaho. Warrants were issued in Utah for the arrest of the parents charging them with "kidnapping" their own son and fleeing the state of Utah. They and their son were brought back to Utah.

The first thing I remembered, was the treatment the learned doctors of his day gave George Washington when he got a cold. The doctors who treated him were agreed that his problem had to be "bad blood". Therefore, they "bled" him to get rid of some of his "bad blood". Nevertheless, he was still sick, so they did it again. The only problem was that he died, so they had to bury him.

It is extremely alarming to learn that doctors have the legal power to tell parents what treatment they *must* have their children given. The doctors may not be God yet. Not *all* doctors agree that the only logical treatment for cancer must be chemotherapy. In a few more years that may be as unpopular and obsolete as "bleeding" is now.

Fortunately Utah dropped their charges against the Jensens to let them live in peace.

GOD BLESS AMERICA!

CHAPTER TWENTY-THREE – MEDICAL DICTATORSHIP?

First, may I say that I honor and appreciate good doctors? Our second son is a medical doctor, a physician and surgeon, and he is a good one. I never cease to thank our Father in Heaven for him, and for his angel wife, and for their marvelous family. He is just as good as he is wise and intelligent. When he was a boy he once set a trap and a rabbit got his foot caught in it, but that rabbit wanted

its freedom so badly that it gnawed off its foot in order to get free. Our son felt so sorry for that rabbit that he never set another trap!

My father's father was a physician and surgeon in Salt Lake City. He was a scientist from birth and a brilliantly intelligent man. The first school he ever attended was the medical college itself, but he was a truly educated man. He always carried a notebook in his pocket and he wrote down everything he ever encountered that he didn't already know.

Several years ago arthritic spurs had invaded my nervous column in the lower third of my spine so badly I was about to give up walking forever. But an excellent surgeon in about a four hour surgery one evening clipped those spurs so marvelously that the next morning I was running up and down those hospital stairs and through their halls like I was a young boy, and I have been walking, running, and jumping ever since.

How marvelous is the knowledge and skill our Father in Heaven has given those marvelous doctors and surgeons. I shall appreciate them forever.

However, my own wife developed breast cancer a few years ago, for which she underwent a mastectomy. As her cancer developed, before surgery, and as we sought to find other ways to secure her healing without chemotherapy after surgery, we encountered a few things that caused us concern.

It had always been my understanding that under the U. S. Constitution every person had the right to speak or write anything he desired, and no one could stop him.

Now, lo and behold, under the legal medical dictatorship that seems to have been granted the American Medical Association only licensed doctors are permitted to say anything at all about medical matters. Anyone else can be prosecuted for practicing medicine without a license.

If Jesus Christ suddenly returned, about next month or next year, and did here and now what he did in Israel two thousand years ago, he'd probably be prosecuted by the medical association for practicing medicine without a license.

I am not sure he would be too happy with that one. Maybe we had better set that one on the back burner, or maybe earmark the whole program for reconsideration.

As a citizen, I am not too excited about seeing any person, or any group of persons, permitted to function as a dictatorship to tell other people what to do and what decisions they may or may not make.

GOD BLESS AMERICA!

CHAPTER TWENTY-FOUR – OUT OF BONDAGE

Not long after we returned to Utah last year, the newspaper reported the number of bankruptcies filed in Utah the preceding year was greater than the bankruptcies filed in any other state in the whole United States.

That rather surprised us for two reasons: First, we had been told that 75% of the population of Utah claimed to be Latter-day Saints, one of whose Articles of Faith declares, "We believe in being *honest*"!

Secondly, President Gordon B. Hinckley, whom Latter-day Saints claim to be the living prophet of God on earth, had told us plainly at General Conference to get out of debt without delay even if we had to exchange our present home for a smaller one to afford the house payments.

Centuries ago the Lord sent Moses to lead the Israelites out of bondage in Egypt. They had come into Egypt willingly enough. They had even been led into bondage without too much resistance. But now, when they decided to leave, that was impossible. Someone else was now making all their decisions for them.

It is interesting to note that when Moses came to lead them out of bondage in Egypt many of the Israelites were as reluctant to follow him as many of our own people are to follow the living prophet today. However, that is where the path of safety lies. He holds the keys. Keep your eye on the prophet - the living prophet, and be quick to follow his directions and we will be led out of bondage today as surely as Moses led the Israelites out of bondage in Egypt! When he says get of out of debt, then **DO IT!**

Most of our prophets have said, "Get out of debt and stay out of debt." Are we following our prophets? That is the best way I know of to avoid being in bondage and since the Lord has so instructed he will enable us to do it. Let us have the faith and yield the obedience. When we plant tomatoes, tomatoes are what we will start harvesting. **So, let's do it!**

GOD BLESS AMERICA!

CHAPTER TWENTY-FIVE –
OBEDIENCE

There are two things to remember about all this. The first is that when we obtain any blessing from God it is *by obedience* to that law upon which it is predicated. (Doctrine & Covenants 130:20-21, emphasis added)

The other was declared by Nephi: "I will go and *do* the things which the Lord hath commanded, for I know that *the Lord giveth no commandments unto the children of men, save he shall prepare a way for them that they may accomplish the thing which he commandeth them.*" (*The Book of Mormon*, I Nephi 3:7, emphasis added)

That is another "law" we had better get memorized if we ever expect to get the motor actually running!

I get the impression we are not taking the Lord very seriously. Do we not remember what the Brother of Jared had to say about this? "And he answered, Yea, Lord, I know that thou speaketh the truth, for thou art a God of truth, and canst not lie."(The Book of Mormon, Ether 3:12) He not only *will* not lie, he *cannot* lie. Anything our Father in Heaven *commands, assigns, calls,* or *asks* us to do, is therefore *possible.* If it was not possible before, it just became possible when he asked us to do it.

That is a "law", so we may as well learn it. When we start obeying the "laws", we start obtaining the blessings that are the fruit of that obedience.

When I was Mission President at Hermosillo, Sonora, Mexico 35 years ago, I called in my two Assistants and said to them, "Elder Marion G. Romney, our Area Authority, says that in this mission at this time every pair of missionaries should be baptizing one family of new converts every week. They will be able to do it, if they follow his directions exactly. You are my Assistants and need to set the example to show the rest of the missionaries how to do it. If that wasn't possible last week, it just became possible when Elder Romney asked us to do it."

It took them one week to get organized. Then each Assistant and his companion baptized one family every week for the rest of their mission.

All twelve million Latter-day Saints will be able to get out of debt in the same manner, as soon as they have the faith to do it. That should end the bankruptcies in the State of Utah and among our people everywhere else as well!

That is the same way we can also learn to do everything else, the Prophet asks us, or assigns us, to do. The prophet tells us *what* to do and we go home and hold a Family Council Meeting to find out *how* to do it and *where to start.* When he tells us what to do it now becomes possible to do it and we do not need to question the commandment we just need to start planning on the method we will use to get it accomplished.

As the Lord said a century and a half ago: "Wherefore, let them bring their families to this land, as they shall counsel among themselves and with me." (Doctrine & Covenants 58:25)

When we do it that way, all twelve million of us will soon be out of debt and bankruptcies will end. That will end this grinding financial recession that is causing so much misery.

The Lord and our Prophet will also tell us what to do to get rain and end this drought, when we get enough faith to listen and pay attention and do what we are asked to do. A good place to start might be with our Sacramental Covenants and with Chapter 26 of the Book of Leviticus. Read it!

Let us do it!

GOD BLESS AMERICA!

CHAPTER TWENTY-SIX –
COMPASSIONATE AND MERCIFUL

John Carter is from North Carolina. One of his brothers is not only a Baptist preacher in North Carolina, but also the director of a School of Divinity there for the training of Baptist preachers.

Attempting to explain to his brother why he had been baptized into The Church of Jesus Christ of Latter-day Saints, John Carter said;

"We have the same basic core beliefs that you have. We believe in God, we believe in Jesus Christ and we believe in the Holy Ghost.

"We believe in the Bible, we believe in faith, and we believe in prayer. We believe all that God has revealed, all that he does now reveal, and we believe that he will yet reveal many great and important things pertaining to the Kingdom of God.

"This Church has come forth as predicted by the Apostle Peter, and much we have received by revelation in our day has been to restore things that were in Christ's Church in the days of Peter, but were lost after the death of the early Apostles, and therefore needed to be restored."

His brother responded, "Such as what?"

Brother Carter replied, "Well, open your Bible. Let us read chapter three of the First Epistle General of the Apostle Peter."

They opened the Bible and read it. Then Brother Carter asked, "What do you understand from verses 18 to 21, which say:

"For Christ also hath once suffered for sins, the just for the unjust, that he might bring us to God, being put to death in the flesh, but quickened by the Spirit; by which also he went and preached unto the spirits in prison; which sometime were disobedient, when once the longsuffering of God waited in the days of Noah, while the ark was a preparing; wherein few, that is, eight souls were saved by water."

"Well, responded his brother, "I hardly know what to think. I had never heard that read before. It almost sounds like he is saying that while Christ's body was in the tomb after his crucifixion his Spirit went and preached to the spirits in prison, which were wicked and rebellious in the day of Noah, but now were being given another chance by our Father in Heaven. I really don't understand it. I'll have to ask our theologian about it."

"You would do better to ask the Lord," replied Brother Carter. You people have not received a revelation from the Lord since the death of the early apostles. That is why the Lord had to restore it by revelation in our day.

So our Father in Heaven sent Jesus Christ to preach to the spirits in prison to give them another chance, after they had rejected the preaching of Noah while the ark was under preparation.

When they rejected Noah in that earlier time, they were wicked and rebellious. Do you know how wicked they really were? The Bible says:

"And God saw that the wickedness of man was great in the earth, and that every imagination of the thoughts of his heart was only evil continually." (The Genesis 6:5, The Holy Bible, p. 9).

Every thought was evil continuously? It is almost difficult to become more wicked than that!

If he even gave *them* a second chance he could not possibly do any less for every other person, who ever breathed the breath of life on this earth. Every person who ever lived will have the fullness of the Gospel of Jesus Christ preached to him, either in this life, in mortality, or in the spirit world after death, or both. Every one - bar none.

That is an encouraging reassurance! What a delightfully joyous thought! It is hard to think about that very long without reaching the conclusion that our Father in Heaven is the most merciful and compassionate Father we ever heard of!

If our Father in Heaven is merciful and kind and compassionate enough to give a second chance even to those who so completely rejected the preaching of Noah, will he not now also grant the petition of the sons and daughters of the pioneers as we now seek to get them to *return to him?*

Invite your wife and your children to join you in prayer as you ask him to help us all get back "on track" that we may enjoy again the peace and joy he desires to give us. That is the place to *start.*

When we return to him, he will return to us and give us health and prosperity, joy and love. He may even send us moisture and make us prosper in this land of promise!

Let us do it! – GOD BLESS AMERICA!

CHAPTER TWENTY-SEVEN – JUICE

As I mixed up a can of frozen cherry berry fruit juice for breakfast, I noticed it was canned and frozen at the Honeydew Canada Foods plant in Mississauga, Ontario, Canada. That is followed by "Canada Law 4P4," which I suppose is the law that had to be complied with for its production.

The next thing that comes to my head is, where in Utah are we doing the same thing? And what about our other states, and the rest of Canada? And Mexico?

What would happen if we raised delicious fruits all over North America, and did it so economically that everyone had all of them they could eat?

We could do that you know. One revelation says, "For the earth is full, and there is enough and to spare." (Doctrine & Covenants 104: 17)

Therefore, we could do it. We are not waiting on the Lord. He is waiting on *us*.

What would we have to do? Well, first, throw off the shackles of taxes, starting with abolishing the taxes on industries. They just add cost to the product and the taxpayer pays for it all anyway, in higher prices.

Then we need to pass the proposed Judicial Constitutional amendment, to put checks and balances on our Federal Judges and our Supreme Court. They have become a huge dictatorship, usurping the powers of our President and our Congress, and we do not even get to *vote* on them.

We need to get back to the Constitution, repeal the Federal Reserve Act of 1913, abolish the Federal Reserve, the IRS, and the Income Tax. We need to have Congress create and control our money like the Constitution says, instead of the banks. Part of the money created by Congress would be used for expenses of government, but only those authorized by the Constitution.

Part would be loaned to the banks at interest, with the banks collecting the interest from whomever borrows the money from the bank.

You may say, "That will never work," but the Lord, and the Constitution, say it will.

GOD BLESS AMERICA!

CHAPTER TWENTY-EIGHT – DEAR FAMILY

Sunday we went to our grandson's ward for the blessing of their beautiful baby boy, Dallin James Olsen. There is another of those choice celestial spirits that got assigned to come down and get this all straightened out after so many confused people have succeeded in getting it into the mass of confusion it is in today. The Founding Fathers are no doubt celebrating to see our Father in Heaven getting around to getting it done.

In the doctor's office, a month ago, there were some interesting statistics:

In 1900 the incidence of cancer in the U. S. was 1 in 30;

In 1980 it was 1 in 5;

In the year 2000 it was 1 in 3;

What is it now? What will it be by the year 2010?

When it gets to 1 in 1 that will mean that everyone in the United States has cancer, or has had it, or will yet get it. Why?

When my wife had her mastectomy, the surgeon who performed it, and the oncologist we were sent to after the operation, both said there is no known cure for cancer and in fact the cause of cancer is not even yet known.

That is not what Lorraine Day (herself a medical doctor) says in her videos "Cancer Doesn't Scare Me Any More" and "You Can't Improve on God".

"There is a law, irrevocably decreed in heaven before the foundations of this world upon which all blessings are predicated –

"And when we obtain any blessing from God it is by obedience to that law upon which it is predicated." (Doctrine & Covenants 130: 20-21)

So when Lorraine Day obtained enough knowledge concerning the laws for the healing of cancer, and obeyed them, she was healed.

We recently heard that Israel passed a law ten years ago eradicating the use of insecticides and pesticides. The instance of cancer in Israel dropped by 50% in the next ten years.

What is the Food and Drug Administration of the U.S. doing about that? The doctors were very insistent that my wife get chemotherapy and radiation, but she declined and instead we decided to do some serious studying.

In her book "The Cure for all Cancers", Hulda Regehr Clark, Ph.D., N.D., says that. "Cancers are caused by a parasite. It is the human intestinal fluke, which typically lives in the intestine, where it might do little harm. But if it invades the uterus or kidneys or liver it does a great deal of harm. If it establishes itself in the liver, it causes cancer. It only establishes itself in the liver of some people. These people have isopropyl alcohol in their bodies. All cancer patients (100%) have both isopropyl alcohol and the intestinal fluke in their livers. The solvent, isopropyl alcohol, is responsible for letting the fluke establish itself in the liver. In order to get cancer, you must have both the parasite and isopropyl alcohol in your body."

Isopropyl alcohol is used in the production of nearly all cosmetics and many foods in the U.S. What is the food and Drug (FDA) doing about that? Are they going to wait until our incidence of cancer is 1 in 1 before they move? And where is our Congress who is supposed to see that all federal agencies are doing their duty?

Where are the voters to make sure we have Congressmen who will do it?

A few years ago a Southern Senator said, "To expect Congress to clean up Congress is like expecting a hog to butcher itself!"

Well, if they will not do it, then the voters must. The Lord says we must diligently seek for our officials men who are wise, good, (men of integrity), and honest (thieves and liars do not qualify, according to the Lord). (Doctrine & Covenants 98:10, p. 190).

Eventually all this will happen, because Moroni has the authority to get it done. (See Chapter 31) However, *we* do not have to wait. So, **let us do it!**

GOD BLESS AMERICA!

CHAPTER TWENTY-NINE – RESIDENCE

My maternal grandparents, from Norway and Denmark, moved to Vernal, Utah early, with other pioneers, to clear and plow the land and help make the wilderness blossom as the rose, as Isaiah had foretold. Within a few years, there were beautiful farms and sweeping alfalfa fields in all directions.

As the next generation arose, they consolidated the gains of their parents and soon there were dairy herds, productive fields, and even a prospering city to beautify the land. Nevertheless, by the next generation things had changed. Fired with the zeal that education produces, this generation was soon off to college getting "degrees" in every field of endeavor.

At a family reunion in Vernal a couple of years ago, which was beautiful, a tour was given of the old homesteads. It was a little sad to think of those who had left the area to obtain college degrees and a university education, and even expressed that disappointment to another cousin, while returning from where he had pointed out the location of our grandparent's earlier log house and corral.

"Yes, he responded, that does cause a little concern, does it not?"

He quickly added, "But did you notice those beautiful homes now replacing the log houses of our grandparents and Aunt Mary? Those are not farmhouses, you will have noticed, but beautiful new city homes.

"Who do you think live in them?" Those very youth who went away to obtain those college degrees! Not much can be done with college degrees in a wheat patch or field of alfalfa, so they moved here and there, all over the nation, and some even abroad, using their talents and abilities to bless the lives of all mankind.

"But now more and more of them are retiring, and moving back where they can live in a crime-free area only twenty minutes from that beautiful new temple!

"They do not even have to get out in storms and blizzards to milk the cows, like you and I had to do when we lived here while attending high school. They have automobiles and can do their shopping in good weather. They can also keep their milk in the refrigerator and let the farmers do the milking!"

Well, what do you know about that? How neat!

Moreover, have you ever heard of "Cities of Zion"? That is even more interesting!

GOD BLESS AMERICA!

CHAPTER THIRTY – UTAH

When Brigham Young gazed out over the barren landscape of the Great Salt Lake valley and considered the harshness of its climate, many of his associates urged him to continue onward to the lush, verdant valleys and pleasant climate of beautiful California ahead. Instead, Brigham Young declared, "If there is any place so bleak and undesirable that no one else wants it, that's where I want to settle my people." And so he did.

He taught his people to build canals and bring the water from the mountains to the valleys below, to make the desert blossom as the rose as the Prophet Isaiah had so long ago foreseen. He sent them north and south and east and west, establishing colonies throughout the whole Rocky Mountain region, and even beyond it. They founded cities and towns and villages from Alberta and British Columbia to Chihuahua and Sonora. They built schools and universities, and factories and plants of every kind. They built roads and highways and freeways, and today the State of Utah and the states and provinces on all sides, stretch forth as a throbbing, thriving, vibrant, empire pressing forth for further expansion all about. Those early pioneers cleared off the brush and tilled the soil and soon orchards and fields spread everywhere.

The next generation solidified the conquests and accomplishments of their parents and rejoiced in the fruits thereof. For a century and a half they multiplied and grew and progressed, at home and abroad. Not only was the inventor of television a Latter-day Saint, but so also have been multitudes of leaders in every other field of human endeavor.

As called and sent by their prophet, thousands of Latter-day Saints have gone forth to fill two year missions all over the earth, as sixty five thousand are doing today. For the percentage of their people who speak at least one foreign language fluently, the Latter-day Saints probably excel all people on earth. Like your own grandparents, mine gathered here, to America, to the Rocky Mountains, and even to Utah, a century and a half ago. Taught that "The Glory of God is Intelligence, or in other words light and truth," they have placed high values on education and on all learning in general.

Their emblem is the beehive, symbolizing the value of work, and willing collaboration and cooperation. They are taught the value of prayer, and to love and serve one another. In my ninety years of observation I have never seen a Latter-day Saint beggar.

I was born in Utah and lived here as a child. Then I lived my youth and adult life in Idaho, Wyoming, Arizona, Texas, Virginia and California and elsewhere, among Latter-day Saints and among non-Latter-day Saints, all wonderful people whom we love and appreciate.

Moving back to Utah a few years ago we were confronted with two great and very apparent needs. The first is the need for water in the horrible drought we were suffering. The second is the grinding poverty of many of our people in this wearisome financial recession through which we are wallowing. Since I am now ninety years old perhaps I could comment on both of these, since I have seen much of them both during my lifetime. But first, let me relate an experience I had when I was about fourteen years old.

We were already in the Great Depression and my father, a school teacher, had left home for several weeks to see if he could find any work to bolster our sagging finances. My sister practiced her violin hour after hour, almost endlessly it seemed to me, and I practiced my trumpet, but a little less enthusiastically I feel obliged to confess.

Fascinated with the idea of constructing an electric motor, I obtained a battery, a few magnets, some coils of wire, and a few other things and set to work. I did some diligent research on the matter, obeyed all the "laws" of this enterprise, and soon, to my great delight, had put together an electric motor that actually ran.

The thrill of this accomplishment was most invigorating, but of even greater worth was the lesson I thereby learned that has stayed in my head and heart ever since: "In any endeavor, we achieve success only as we obey those laws on which that success is predicated." Or as it says in one revelation in this latter-day Restoration, "There is a law, irrevocably decreed in heaven before the foundations of this world, upon which all blessings are predicated. And when we obtain any blessing from God, it is by obedience to that law upon which it is predicated." (Doctrine & Covenants 130: 20-21)

That fascinates me. We can have any cake we choose to bake. All we have to do is find the recipe, and follow it closely, and the cake is ours. That is as certain as if it had been cut in cement or rock, but you have to believe it, and then to obey it, before it does you any good!

Let's start on drought, a problem we have had off and on in San Diego for many years. We had endured so many droughts in San Diego we had just come to accept it as a problem for which there was no solution, but several years ago, while in our fifth year of severe drought, one Sunday our Bishop asked us to fast the next Sunday and pray for rain.

So we did. We fasted and we prayed for rain. And we *got* it – about ten drops! So naturally we all said, "Too bad! But that's just the way things are. Maybe we don't deserve anything better!" Our Bishop really got on our case. He told us how serious our problem was and said if we did not get rain soon lettuce would be costing $5.00 a head, if you could get it all.

Then he told us our Area President had asked the Stake Presidents to tell our Bishops to tell us to get serious about this and stop playing around with it, like it was some kind of a game. So the next Sunday we fasted and prayed again, but this time we *really* fasted and *really* prayed and we got our rain, over one inch of it, which is a lot of water in a place as dry as San Diego!

About a week later our Bishop told us our Area President, Elder John H. Groberg, had held a meeting with all our Stake Presidents and told them:

"If the Latter-day Saints will keep the commandments of the Lord and especially keep the Sabbath Day holy, when they fast and pray and ask for rain, the Lord will send the rain without any regard whatsoever of how worthy or unworthy anyone else may be!" Maybe Utah will have to start doing it that way to get some rain! We could also consider that to be a "law".

And who is Elder John H. Groberg? He's the one who raised a boy from the dead, when he was a missionary in Tonga! So he knows the power of faith and what it can do! Of course to get Latter-day Saints who would qualify for these blessings they might have to clean us up a bit and get us to repent and obey the Lord, and also obey the Prophet while we are at it!

Anciently, the Lord made a covenant with Father Lehi: "Inasmuch as thy seed keep my commandments they shall *prosper* in the Land of Promise! BUT, if they do *not* keep my commandments they shall be *cut off* from the presence of the Lord." (Alma 9:13)

What happens then? We grieve the Holy Ghost and he departs from us and we lose the privilege of revelation from our Father in Heaven, and we are turned over to the buffetings of Satan. That "gift of the Holy Ghost" is really a marvelous gift, when you stop to think about it. When I used to read in the Book of Mormon that the early Nephites received "many revelations" I used to think it said "daily". Actually it is even better than that, we can receive them any time we *need* them.

When we need to remember something that has slipped our mind and we pray about it and it is brought back to our memory, is that not *revelation* by the Holy Ghost? When we have lost something and we pray about it and the Holy Ghost tells us where to look for it, is not that revelation also?

When we were building a house and the Spirit said, "Duck!" and we quickly obeyed and escaped getting clobbered, wasn't that also revelation? What a wonderful gift is the gift of the Holy Ghost! When we comprehend what a marvelous gift it is, will we not be eager to keep the Sabbath Day holy and be diligent in obeying our sacramental covenants to remember our Savior, Jesus Christ always, and keep all of his commandments and always follow his direction?

There are two things to remember about the Lord's covenant with Father Lehi. First, it carried *no expiration date*. It is still valid. It is still in effect. Secondly, Father Lehi said the Gentiles brought to this land by the Lord *would be considered his seed and would be blessed with his seed as they keep the commandments of the Lord.* So why don't we now claim that blessing by qualifying for it?

The revelation says that before the Second Coming of Jesus Christ "the Lamanites shall blossom as the rose." (Doctrine & Covenants 49:24) Is that part of the blessing *we* are to get with the seed of Lehi when we qualify for it?

Why don't we ask for it? And can't the rose blossom better with *more water*, and maybe even *more_money* to go with it? Why don't we ask for those also? We have to remember that everything we get we must obtain through the "law of the harvest." If we plant radishes, radishes are what we're going to get, and not tomatoes! Maybe it is time to plant some *tomatoes*!

How about it, Utah? How would you like to receive abundant moisture, to convert our whole state into a beautiful garden and save us from this depressing drought? And how about some prosperity to go with it? "And inasmuch as thy seed shall keep my commandments they shall prosper upon the land of promise." That is still in effect, and it still includes us as well as Lehi's own children. It includes abundance of food and clothing, a good bed to sleep in, a good home, and money enough to pay for them. It also includes health, happiness, and love at home.

"And the Lord said…, Wherefore did Sarah laugh? … Is anything too hard for the Lord?" (Genesis 18:13-14)

Our Heavenly Father can do all things. The only thing he cannot do is to lie: "For thou art a God of truth and canst not lie" (*The Book of Mormon*, Ether 3:12)

When we keep his commandments, we are pure in heart and filled with faith, and when we are filled with faith, we receive every blessing we pray for, including rain!

GOD BLESS AMERICA!

CHAPTER THIRTY-ONE – CITIES OF ZION

On page ninety-one of the book "The Restored Church by William Edwin Berrett, you will find the Plan for the City of Zion prepared by Joseph Smith for the city then planned for formation at Independence, Missouri, to be known as the City of Zion. This was to serve as a model for other cities to be built round about until they filled the earth.

Unlike the sprawling cities of today with millions of inhabitants so densely packed, they have no room for a garden. In these cities of Zion, the city itself would be one mile square, surrounded by another one mile area on all sides, for farming and a zoned "wilderness area". Each family would have a one-half acre lot with gardens, fruit trees, and berry bushes sufficient to feed their family. When the population reached 20,000, another city would be formed.

Under the Law of Consecration, over-all property ownership would be by the group with individual homes, businesses, etc., deeded to the families as a stewardship, but only what they could handle.

It would all be freewill and cooperative, as it is now, but eventually it will work like the city of Enoch. There will be no idlers there, and with that much gardening to do, probably no one will consider himself very much "unemployed"!

Organize yourselves...See that ye love one another; cease to be covetous; learn to impart one to another as the gospel requires.

Cease to be idle; cease to be unclean; cease to find fault one with another...

And above all things, clothe yourselves with the bond of charity, as with a mantel, which is the bond of perfect ness and peace.

Pray always, that ye may not faint, until I come. Behold, and lo, I will come quickly, and receive you unto myself. Amen. (Doctrine & Covenants 88:119-126)

One of the great assignments we have received is to fully establish Zion by the Lord's standards, and prepare the Lord's people for his Second Coming. He will do the reigning, but we are to do the preparing. Moreover, the first thing to be prepared is His *people.*

In the Cities of Zion, we will have temples and everything else we need to teach, train, and prepare our people. Our cities will be crime-free because our people are crime-free.

The Constitution will be restored, and we will live by it. Our laws will be just because our lawmakers are just. Our lawmakers will be just because our voters are just and they obey the commandments of the Lord to diligently seek for our leaders, men who are wise, just (men of integrity), and honest. Leaders, who are honest, are neither thieves nor liars.

Before we will be able to live Celestial laws enough to qualify as the Zion of the Lord, we must be ready to live the United Order, sometimes called the Order of Enoch. That will require teaching and training, including the teaching that is going on right now, as well as that to be carried out after Cities of Zion are established.

At a Stake Conference in Shelley, Idaho in 1935, Elder Joseph

Fielding Smith told us of a man from Ogden, who had recently come to visit him in his office. The man asked, "Brother Smith, when will the Church be living the United Order again?"

"I don't know," answered Elder Smith, "How much do you have to invest in it?"

"I do not have anything," replied the man, "That is why I asked."

"Are you a full tithe-paper?" Elder Smith asked.

"Well no, Brother Smith," replied the visitor. "This is a full depression and it is all I can do to put food on the table to keep my family from starving to death!"

"Well," responded Elder Smith, "When the Church again lives the United Order no one will be invited to participate who is not a full tithe-payer." Therefore, you see, we are already in the process of preparation, right now.

To live in Cities of Zion will be a joyous experience for those who are prepared and have the faith, courage, and enthusiasm for it!

Holy Father, grant us thy Holy Spirit to lead us safely in the way of the Lord, and make us worthy to stand in the presence of the Savior when He comes in the clouds of glory!

GOD BLESS AMERICA!

CHAPTER THIRTY-TWO – MORONI

Elder Orson Hyde is the Apostle who was sent to Jerusalem 160 years ago to dedicate the land of Israel for the return of the Jews. If you want to read something interesting read the Independence Day discourse of Elder Hyde given in the Salt Lake City Tabernacle on July 4, 1854. A photocopy of it is held from pages 369 to 371 of Volume 6 of the Journal of Discourses.

After speaking for a while about the Independence of the United States and the valor of those who accomplished it, Elder Hyde talks about Moroni, the heavenly messenger sent to tell Joseph Smith about the Book of Mormon.

Moroni, he said, is the "Guardian Angel" of the United States. He was at the side of George Washington through the whole Revolutionary War, telling him what to do and how to do it, and keeping him from being killed.

Moroni was at the side of Christopher Columbus as he crossed the Ocean, telling him what to do and how to do it, through visions and inspired dreams.

Moroni has another important assignment yet to fulfill. He has been assigned to return, in the due time of the Lord, to *restore* our Constitution. The more you think about that the more significant it becomes.

In the first place, we must have already had a Constitutional apostasy or Moroni would not have been assigned to *restore* it.

Secondly, if it is his assignment to *restore* it, it must be important for us to help get it done, and to be involved in preparing for it!

Our Constitution must be *important*, for the Lord to assign an angel to restore it!

GOD BLESS AMERICA!

CHAPTER THIRTY-THREE –
RECAPITULATION AND SUMMARY

This author, a retired Special Agent of the J. Edgar Hoover, F. B. I., and active member of The Church of Jesus Christ of Latter-day Saints is alone responsible for this book and everything in it.

In his opinion, the Supreme Court committed three violations of the Constitution in their action of 1962 rewriting the Compulsory Education Law to bar prayer, The Bible, the Ten Commandments and God from Public Schools.

He proposes a Judicial Supreme Court Amendment to correct this error and proposes that all parents be permitted to send their children to any school of their choice. Since the parents are taxpayers, he proposes the dollars follow the student.

He also proposes the repeal of the 16th and 17th Amendments and the Federal Reserve Act of 1913, and the abolishment of the Federal Reserve Bank, I.R.S., and Federal Income Tax.

He proposes our monetary system be corrected to comply with Constitutional provisions requiring Congress to create and control our money instead of the Banks. Inasmuch as the money would then be already in the hands of the Government, ready to be spent, there would be no further need for either the Federal Income Tax or the I.R.S. to collect it.

Federal Reserve Chairman, Alan Greenspan proposes cooling our economy and reducing our supply of money to avoid inflation, which he says is caused by too much money chasing too few goods.

This author proposes reversing this equation to double our money and quadruple our production of goods. Relieved of present confiscatory powers of taxation our citizens would have the means to establish plants and industries all over our nation to produce in abundance everything we could possibly need or use. Everyone willing to work would be employed, every family would have an income, and the multitudes now preparing tax returns could serve as supervisors, directors and administrators of our plants and industries throughout our nation. Then we would really prosper!

Churches and all other organizations and individuals should be totally free to express any opinion they desire concerning any matter, including politics, as already guaranteed by the Constitution.

The God-given right to the creation and possession of property should be sustained totally as guaranteed by the Constitution. The government should refrain from plundering its citizens and seizing their property to give to individuals or anyone else, inasmuch as this is not authorized by the Constitution.

The Lord has promised His protection not only to the Gentiles who gathered to this land to establish this nation, but also to this nation itself as long as the people thereof are faithful to our Father in Heaven and keep the commandments of God.

This nation is a constitutional Republic rather than a Democracy. It is controlled by God and its constitution whereas an unrestricted democracy is free at any time to do anything the majority of the voters demand, even if what they demand is obviously evil and is destructive to the nation and its people.

The Tenth Amendment limits the powers of the Federal Government to those powers specifically granted in the Constitution and requires all other powers to be left in the hands of the States and the people. Initially, members of the House of Representatives were chosen by the vote of the Citizens in their congressional district, as is done today. Initially, however, their State Government, appointed the Senators, and hired and fired them and set their pay. Their function was to *represent their state in preventing the Federal Government from usurping powers that should have remained in the hands of the States.* The Seventeenth Amendment required Senators to be elected by the vote of all voters in their state. They no longer seem to represent the needs of their states and this appears to nullify the Tenth Amendment.

It is pointed out that it might be more advisable to have the Federal Government pay more attention to those functions specifically assigned to them by the constitution, such as the common defense and related matters, rather than teaching farmers to plow and children to read and write and do basic math, *neither of which appear authorized in the Constitution.*

The promised protection of the Lord to the Gentiles gathered to this land was largely fulfilled in the 1746 destruction of the French fleet sent to burn Boston to the ground. This deliverance was obtained through the faith, prayers, and fasting of the Colonists, appealing to God for His deliverance. Boston was saved and not one shot was fired.

Restoring our Constitution and maintaining it faithfully would abolish our taxes, promote the General Welfare, and make this Nation the greatest, most powerful, and most prosperous nation on earth. The Bible declares that God requires those who govern in governments be men of honor and integrity, and when the citizens of our land become a nation of integrity, our leaders and our government will be likewise, and we will truly be blessed of the Lord. When we do that, other nations will follow our example, as our Father in Heaven intended and desires.

GOD BLESS AMERICA!

About the Author

Eugene Foss Olsen retired from the FBI after more than 25 years of service as a Special Agent. He and his wife, Rae are the parents of 6 children, 61 grandchildren and over 116 great-grandchildren.

Eugene has been a Patriarch in The Church of Jesus Christ of Latter-day Saints for over 43 years, serving in both English and Spanish. In his youth he was a missionary in the Spanish-American Mission. He served as President of the Mexico West Mission from 1967 to 1971. He also served as interim Mission President of the Bolivia Santa Cruz Mission and the Bolivia La Paz Mission, and has held many other Church callings through the years.

Eugene was called to serve as a full-time Regional Representative of The Council of the Twelve Apostles in the Andes Area from 1979 through 1983 serving in Peru, Ecuador, Bolivia, and Colombia. He was then called as the first Temple President of the Santiago Chile Temple in 1982 by President Gordon B. Hinckley. Eugene passed away August 18, 2011.

Other books by this author

Please visit your favorite ebook retailer to discover other books by Eugene Foss Olsen:

We Believe The Bible!

Truth and Consequences

www.ingramcontent.com/pod-product-compliance
Lightning Source LLC
Chambersburg PA
CBHW060413290526
45791CB00002B/735